Community College Movement in Perspective

Teachers College Responds to the Truman Commission

Martin S. Quigley
Thomas W. Bailey

A SCARECROWEDUCATION BOOK

The Scarecrow Press, Inc.
Lanham, Maryland, and Oxford
2003

A SCARECROWEDUCATION BOOK

Published in the United States of America
by Scarecrow Press, Inc.
A Member of the Rowman & Littlefield Publishing Group
4501 Forbes Boulevard, Suite 200, Lanham, Maryland 20706
www.scarecroweducation.com

PO Box 317
Oxford
OX2 9RU, UK

British Library Cataloguing in Publication Information Available

Library of Congress Cataloging-in-Publication Data

Quigley, Martin, 1917–
  Community college movement in perspective : Teachers College responds
to the Truman Commission / Martin S. Quigley, Thomas W. Bailey.
     p. cm
  ISBN 0-8108-4538-5 (hardback : alk. paper)
  1. Community colleges—United States—History. I. Bailey, Thomas W.,
1950– II. Title.
  LB2328.15.U6 Q54 2003
  378.1'543'0973—dc21
                                                          2002011390

⊗™ The paper used in this publication meets the minimum requirements of
American National Standard for Information Sciences—Permanence of
Paper for Printed Library Materials, ANSI/NISO Z39.48-1992.
Manufactured in the United States of America.

Contents

Preface

This book was written for two useful and interrelated reasons: The lack of understanding, at the time and since, of the importance of President Truman's Commission recommendation in 1947 for the U.S. establishment of public postsecondary institutions, called for the first time "community colleges," and little appreciation of the enduring role played by Teachers College of Columbia University in the community-college movement from the beginning and continuing into the foreseeable future.

I had the privilege of graduating from Teachers College under the tutelage of two giants of the community-college movement: Walter E. Sindlinger and Michael Brick. I have known for more than a quarter of a century another significant figure, Joseph Hankin, president of Westchester Community College in Purchase, New York, who taught regularly at Teachers College through the years. During my final year as a student, I served as Dr. Sindlinger's administrative assistant.

Some critics might object that the creator of this project has never taught or worked as an administrator in a community college. This is true. I took all of the necessary coursework to be qualified in the community-college field, but I elected to write a dissertation in the area of higher-education administration, "The Government Relations of the Five Universities in Washington, D.C." Donna Shalala and Dr. Sindlinger were the principal dissertation sponsors.

My credentials are of another sort. My mother and an aunt were students at the Lewis Institute (later the Illinois Institute of Technology), a contender with the Joliet Illinois Junior College for bragging rights—along with a few other institutions—as being the first junior college.

One of my sisters attended another type of two-year postsecondary institution, Georgian Court in New Jersey, at the time a finishing school run by nuns.

During my fifteen years of teaching graduate courses (mostly as an adjunct, for I was—and still am—an executive of a small, specialized, publishing company and the writer of a number of books), I taught a variety of courses to community college teachers and administrators at Seton Hall, Baruch College of the University of the City of New York, and at Teachers College, lastly, as a visiting professor.

My major qualification for composing this book is that I have had, from my earliest days as an education graduate student, a deep appreciation for the importance of community colleges and a keen awareness that an understanding of these colleges is lacking in many circles, including some in education. Too often people regard community colleges as "junior" in ways that have nothing to do with two-year programs leading to an associate's degree. Such attitudes have fostered, in some places and among some individuals, an inferiority complex. These feelings affect teachers, students, and the public being served by community colleges.

In reality, all of those involved in the community-college movement, from its earliest days to the present, should hold their heads high. Community colleges are a twentieth-century American education success story. As we move ahead into the twenty-first century, our community colleges will soon be teaching half or more than half of the postsecondary students. At present, almost half of past high-school students are in community colleges rather than in the four-year colleges and universities which receive most of the attention and monies.

Harry Truman is mostly remembered for his decision to drop the atomic bombs on Hiroshima and Nagasaki. Yet, arguably, his decision to create the President's Commission for Higher Education in a democracy—and to support the recommendations made in the report of the Higher Education Commission in six slim volumes printed in 1947 by the U.S. Government Printing Office—was a decision of more lasting importance. Millions of Americans (and large numbers of peoples overseas) have benefited enormously from a key recommendation of the Truman Commission: the establishment of community colleges.

Teachers College (TC) enthusiastically responded to the call to advance the community-college movement. As Lawrence Cremin, historian and future TC president, wrote a few years after the Truman Commission, "Teachers College was responding to the community college movement with leadership just as it had when public high schools first began to be a major force in American education. . . . In view of the mushrooming junior college movement, it has not been at all surprising to see the college's Division of Instruction giving focal attention to the needs of teachers seeking more effective tools for education at that level."

Arthur Levine, president of Teachers College, in the year 2000 expressed the point this way: "Teachers College shaped the community college movement following the Truman Commission. Moving now into the twenty-first century, Teachers College hopes to continue to provide leadership in scholarship, teaching, and research for the community-college field." This was pointed out by Teachers College's president, Dr. Arthur Levine, in the introduction to this book.

Martin S. Quigley

Acknowledgments

The authors wish to express special thanks to the following:

Joseph S. Brosnan, vice president for Development and External Affairs at Teachers College; and to colleagues in that department who served as project coordinators, Laura Ellis and Nicholas Gulde; David Ment and Bette Weneck, Special Collections Division of the Teachers College Milbank Memorial Library; Paul M. Cartelli, cover design; Diane Dobry, photography; Kathryn D. Oliver, Patrick Rimassa, Terri Ruiz, and Mary Messina for research and editing biographies and dissertation listings; and Loretta Daniele, word processor.

Introduction

This book is about two-year colleges. It is also a volume about the power of a federal commission to reimagine higher education and the place that two-year colleges might play in the future. It is also a book about the role of Teachers College in the expansion of community colleges after World War II. But it is something much more fundamental. It is at once a celebration of an idea, its transformation and phenomenal growth, and the people and institutions that made it possible. It proves that ideas can be powerful and have dramatic consequences. It is also a paean to the American dream, the democratization of education, the commitment to expand opportunity, and the multiplication of colleges catering to those ignored by traditional higher education.

The problem in retelling history is that there seems to be an element of inevitability. Whatever happened was destined to occur. If it didn't happen in one way, it would have happened in another. If it did not happen at the time it occurred, it would have happened a few years later. If the people who made the event happen did not come along, then someone else would have.

This destiny just isn't so. The Truman Commission report was a radical departure from all that came before it. In a nation that was male dominated, segregated, anti-Semitic, and anti-Catholic, with deep pockets of urban and rural poverty, the report called for the end of barriers to higher education based on race, gender, religion, income, and geographic location. In a country in which less than 10% of the college-age population was attending higher education institutions, the Truman Commission said a majority of Americans was capable of enrolling. In a time in which the United States had barely crossed the border between elite and mass access to college, the Truman Commission required nothing less than tuition-free, universal access to college.

Equally astounding was the primary vehicle the Commission chose to achieve these goals. It was the junior college, which they called the community college. (This decision was not wholly dissimilar from Cinderella's fairy godmother turning a pumpkin into an elegant carriage and rats into footmen. This fate does not actually happen in real life, only in fairy tales.) The junior college was created as a castoff. The president of the University of Chicago wanted to make his school a true German-type or a Johns Hopkins–like university. In order to accomplish this, he decided that Chicago had to unload its lower division program, in other words its freshman and sophomore years, which, in his opinion, fit better within the high school. When the Joliet, Illinois, public school system accepted his hand-me-down, a new institution was born, the junior college. In its earliest years, junior-college students were more affluent than their peers attending state universities and the only curricula offered were liberal arts, university transfer programs. In the years after World War I, vocational and nontransfer programs grew and the population attending declined.

By the time of the Truman Commission, the two-year colleges, which numbered more than six hundred, were confused in mission and faced an uncertain future. The Commission did nothing less than imagine a crystal-clear purpose and future for them, which made community colleges the keystone of higher education. These community colleges were institutions tied to the educational needs of their communities, with access for all Americans to higher education. It was a shear act of imagination by the Commission. In no sense of the word was the choice inevitable. The Truman Commission proposal for two-year colleges was as radical as its vision of higher education.

Extraordinarily, the vision came to fruition. Today 65% of all high-school graduates attend some form of postsecondary education. There are more than 1,200 community colleges in the United States, and they are the most frequently used approach to college for the nation's college-bound students. These schools enroll a disproportionate share of America's minority, economically disadvantaged, part-time, and first generation college students.

These changes did not occur immediately upon the release of the Commission's report. They took decades. They required an evolution of the American economy, departing farther and farther from agriculture to industry and then an information base, which necessitated more and more education for our citizenry. This need encouraged the states to expand their higher education systems, to build more colleges (including significant investments in community colleges), and to create master plans that guided the development of their higher education systems of which community colleges were often the open door. The expansion of community colleges also required an end to segregation, a Civil Rights and women's movements, and an equal rights amendment in order to reduce the barriers of race, religious, and gender discrimination. The Truman Commission necessitated a Great Society program, which provided financial aid and preparatory programs for the nation's disadvantaged to attend college. They provided the dream and the map for accomplishing the Great Society's vision of higher education.

One more thing was necessary—the expertise to enact the Truman Commission's vision. It is here that Teachers College (TC) played a part. TC embraced the community college as an important direction for the future of higher education and gave its name and its reputation to the movement. TC hired faculty who were experts or became experts in community colleges. Over the years, TC prepared two-year college curricula and programs, educated faculty and administrators to staff community colleges, educated scholars to study community colleges, and engaged in research, publications, and conferences on critical community-college issues. Today Professor Thomas W. Bailey operates a renowned community-college research center at Teachers College, Professor Kevin Dougherty writes about the community college and educates graduate students who will lead them in TC's higher-education program, Professor Delores Perrin focuses on issues of developmental education at two-year colleges, and President Joseph Hankin of Westchester Community College teaches our students about the world in which he is one of the leading practitioners. There is a long history of community-college work at Teachers College. There is also an important and vital future in research on the seminal issues in community-college education, the preparation of future leaders for America's community colleges, and the education of the current community-college leaders, as well as helping to shape the national debate and policy on community-college education and working with community colleges on current practice.

I congratulate Martin S. Quigley for deciding that it was necessary to write a book about the Truman Commission, the community college movement, and Teachers College. I am grateful to him and Thomas W. Bailey for producing this volume. They have written a much needed, too long absent volume about one of the great turning points in American higher education.

Arthur Levine
President, Teachers College

The Truman Commission

Less than a year after the atomic bombs dropped on Hiroshima and Nagasaki, on July 13, 1946, President Harry S. Truman established the President's Commission on Higher Education. George F. Zook, distinguished educator, was named chairman. Members included educators, prominent churchmen, and well-known citizens. (See the following chart for names of the members of the Commission.)

The Committee's mandate as set by Truman was very broad: "We should now reexamine our system of higher education in terms of its objectives, methods, and facilities; and in the light of the social role it has to play." The first of the specific challenges put to the Commission comprised the "Ways and means of expanding educational opportunities for all able young people." "The President may have an idea which led the Commission's members to the strong recommendation for the establishment everywhere of what they called 'community colleges.'" Truman's Letter of Appointment included "The desirability of establishing a series of intermediate technical institutes."

Truman's final words in his letter of appointment dated July 13, 1946, gave the Commission "free rein": "These topics of inquiry are merely suggestive and not intended to limit in any way the scope of the Commission's work."

President's Commission on Higher Education

George F. Zook, *Chairman*

Sarah G. Blanding
O. C. Carmichael
Arthur H. Compton
Henry Dixon
Milton S. Eisenhower
John R. Emens
Alvin C. Eurich
Douglas S. Freeman
Algo D. Henderson
Msgr. Frederick G. Hochwalt
Lewis W. Jones
Horace M. Kallen
Fred J. Kelly
Murray D. Lincoln

T. R. McConnell
Earl J. McGrath
Martin R. P. McGuire
Agnes Meyer (Mrs. Eugene)
Harry K. Newburn
Bishop G. Bromley Oxnam
F. D. Paterson
Mark Starr
George S. Stoddard
Harold H. Swift
Ordway Tead
Goodrich C. White
Rabbi Stephen S. Wise

Francis J. Brown, *Executive Secretary*
A. B. Bonds Jr., *Assistant Executive Secretary*

CHAPTER 1

The U.S. Scene in 1947

The year after the end of World War II found our nation facing—in the words of President Truman to his Commission on Higher Education— "a period of trial." The Commission's mandate was to address how the problems facing the institutions of higher education should be addressed. The Commission's conclusion was that the existing institutions, even expanded to the greatest degree possible, would be inadequate. The most significant conclusion of the Commission was that a large number of two-year public institutions needed to be created. The Commission called these institutions "community colleges."

President Truman focused on the needs of the huge number of men and women returning to civilian life from service in the armed forces. The higher education needs to be addressed, of course, were much broader. Naturally veterans were the first priority, but the members of the Commission recognized that research resulting from tests given to millions of servicemen and women showed convincingly that half of the high-school graduates were qualified for at least two years of college-level instruction. Prior to 1940, only about 8% of high-school graduates went on to college. The loss of higher education to millions of qualified students was a personal loss, curtailing individuals' earning power and intellectual development. The loss was both to the individual and to the country as a whole.

In 1946 and the immediately following years, the country was going through the greatest economic retooling in world history. The great production capacity of the United States focused on making war material for the Allies. Not only was it necessary to transfer millions of workers in manufacturing plants to the production of peacetime products but it was also essential to find employment for the veterans. Another tremendous drain on national resources was the looming need to help our Allies and former enemy countries rebuild after the destruction of war years.

Competing with higher education's construction needs were the demands for more housing. Everything required for the expansion of colleges and universities or to erect new institutions—such as community colleges—was also required for the residential market. Money, of course, was an overriding problem. The government had financed the cost of the war to a great extent by the sale of bonds. Advocates for school building in the postwar years had to compete in a very tight credit market.

In addition, the threats posed by the growing difficulties with the Soviet Union—which led to the Cold War—were a factor that kept national interest from focusing on the needs of higher education.

These factors confirm that the Truman Commission on Higher Education operated in a national atmosphere that was not especially focused on students and the problems of institutions serving young people. All this is present in the excellent report in 1947 of the Truman Commission, including its recommendation for community colleges, so outstanding.

The President's Commission on Higher Education operated in a climate where the Administration and Congress had made clear their recognition of the educational needs of returning veterans. Public Laws 16 and the Veterans Rehabilitation Act (collectively known as "The G.I. Bill of Rights") were aimed at facilitating additional higher education through financial grants.

While estimating a doubling of enrollments from the levels of the 1947–1948 academic year within a decade, the Commission wanted social needs addressed. "No thinking person doubted that we are living in a decisive moment in history." The Commission urged that we should not forget the past but must prepare for the future. This would require attention to the needs of a diverse, multicultural society, which should be more international in outlook in the atomic age. "Education is needed to insure equal liberty and equal opportunity. Education is indispensable to the maintenance and growth of freedom of thought, faith, enterprise, and association," the Commission noted.

To suggest how rapidly the education needs of the country were expanding, the Commission estimated that in 1900 students in high schools numbered only seven hundred thousand, or 11% of the school-age population. But in 1940, there were seven million high-school students, 73% of that population. In 1900 college students numbered only 250,000 or 4% of the age cohort. In 1940 there were about 1,500,000 high-school students in college, up to 16% from 1900. In 1947—the year of the Commission's report—the college population was 2,354,000 (of whom about one million were veterans). Even now, with the 2000 U.S. populations of 281,421,906, the Census Bureau estimates that there are almost seventeen million Americans with six years of schooling or less. Of that number, nine million never had any formal schooling or stopped before the end of the fifth grade.

At the time the report was written, about 1,600,000 (or 19%) of eighteen- and nineteen-year-olds were not in school. Turning to the financial barriers that kept so many from continuing their education, the Commission stated that half of the children in 1945 were growing up in families with an annual income of $2,500 or less. Further, it was noted that college-level education was not free and that from 1939 to 1947 college tuition had risen 30%, a fact that made post-high-school education impossible for a large number of young people. A telling observation is that there is little or no relationship between the ability to benefit from a college education and the ability to pay for it. In other words, the students who had relatively affluent parents could go on to higher education; the less wealthy or poor could not afford postsecondary education.

The summary comment of the Truman Commission on the financial impact of post-high-school education is as follows: "By allowing the opportunity for higher education to depend so largely on the individual's economic status, we are not only denying to millions of young people the chance in life to which they are entitled, we are also depriving the nation of a vast amount of potential leadership."

The Commission paid special attention to the Negro (back in 1947 that term was not only acceptable but was a preferred one for those now called African Americans). In 1947 the Commission reported that 11% of the whites aged twenty or older had had at least a year of college but only

3% of blacks had achieved even a year of post-high-school studies. At that time, 5% of whites had finished college but less than 1% of blacks.

The Commission issued an eloquent call for universally available free education for two years beyond the high school's twelfth grade:

> The time has come to make education through the fourteenth grade available in the same way that high school education is now available.
>
> This means that tuition-free education should be available in public institutions to all youth for the traditional freshman and sophomore years or for the traditional two-year junior college course.
>
> To achieve this, it will be necessary to develop much more extensively than at present such opportunities as are now provided in local communities by the two-year junior college, community institute, community college, or institute of arts and sciences. The name used does not matter, though community colleges seems to describe these schools best; the important thing is that the services they perform be recognized and vastly extended.
>
> Such institutions make post-high-school education available to a much larger percentage of young people than otherwise could afford it. Indeed, as discussed in the volume of this Commission's report, "Organizing Higher Education," such community colleges probably will have to carry a large part of the responsibility for expanding opportunities in higher education.
>
> The time has come to provide financial assistance to competent students in the tenth through fourteenth grades who would not be able to continue without such assistance.
>
> Tuition costs are not the major economic barrier to education, especially in college. Costs of supplies, board, and room, and other living needs are great. Even many high-school students are unable to continue in school because of these costs.
>
> Arrangements must be made, therefore, to provide additional financial assistance for worthy students who need it if they are to remain in school. Only in this way can we counteract the effect of family incomes so low that even tuition-free schooling is a financial impossibility for their children. Only in this way can we make sure that all who are to participate in democracy are adequately prepared to do so.

The Truman Commission's report was published in six thin volumes averaging only a few dozen pages each. Why they were published in that way by the Government Printing Office in Washington, D.C., is a mystery today. One likely explanation is that after all of the wartime pressures and shortages of paper and bookbinding supplies, in December 1947 the Printing Office found it more efficient to produce six booklets rather than binding all six in one volume. It may be noted that volume 1, "Establishing the Goals," was published on December 15th. The second volume was published one week later, "Equalizing and Expanding Individual Opportunity." For those interested in community colleges, volume 3, subtitled "Organizing Higher Education," is the most significant.

The preface to volume 3 includes a paragraph showing the importance of the junior college, which was to be named community college, to the members of the Commission: "The increase in the number of community colleges, the influence of this development upon established institutions, the role of the Government, both State and Federal, and the function of voluntary organizations all call for careful appraisal in the organizational development of higher education over the years ahead." Community college was the major subject of chapter 2 of volume 3 which had the title, "Developing Adequate Facilities."

Until recently college education was for the very few. Now a fifth of our young people continue their education beyond the high school.

Many young people want less than a full four-year college course. The two-year college—that is the thirteenth and fourteenth years of our educational system—is about as widely needed today as the four-year high school was a few decades ago. Such a college must fit into the community life as the high school has done.

Hence the President's Commission suggests the name "community college" to be applied to the institution designed to serve chiefly local community education needs. It may have various forms of organization and may have curricula of various lengths. Its dominant feature is its intimate relations to the life of the community it serves.

Essential Characteristics of the Community College

First, the community college must make frequent surveys of its community so that it can adapt its program to the educational needs of its full-time students. These needs are both general and vocational. To this end it should have effective relationships not only with the parents of the students, but with cultural, civic, industrial, and labor groups as well.

These contacts should often take the form of consultative committees which work with faculty personnel. On the basis of such surveys and consultations its program should constantly evolve and never be allowed to become static.

Second, since the program is expected to serve a cross section of the youth population, it is essential that consideration be given not only to apprentice training but also to cooperative procedures which provide for the older students alternate periods of attendance at college and remunerative work. The limited experience which colleges have had over the past three decades with this cooperative method has tended to confirm the belief that there is much educational value in a student's holding a job during his college days, particularly if that job is related to the courses being studied in college.

Third, the community college must prepare its students to live a rich and satisfying life, part of which involves earning a living. To this end, the total educational effort, general and vocational, of any student must be a well-integrated single program, not two programs. The sharp distinction which certain educators tend to make between general or liberal or cultural education on the one hand and vocational or semiprofessional or professional education on the other hand is not valid. Problems which industrial, agricultural, or commercial workers face today are only in part connected with the skills they use in their jobs. Their attitudes and their relationships with others are also important. Certainly the worker's effectiveness in dealing with family, community, national, and international problems, and his interests in maintaining and participating in wholesome recreation programs are important factors in a satisfying life. Many workers should be prepared for membership on municipal government councils, on school boards, on recreation commissions, and the like. The vocational aspect of one's education must not, therefore, tend to segregate "workers" from "citizens."

Fourth, the community college must meet the needs also of those of its students who will go on to a more extended general education or to specialized and professional study at some other college or university. Without doubt, higher education has given a disproportionate amount of attention to this group in the past, and it is well that a more balanced program to serve the needs of larger numbers is in prospect. On the other hand, it must always be kept in mind that one of its primary functions is to lay a firm foundation in general education.

Fifth, the community college must be the center for the administration of a comprehensive adult education program. This is discussed at some length in "Equalizing and Expanding Individual Opportunity," and a statement on organization in connection with adult education is made in Chapter VI of the present volume. It is of utmost importance that the community college recognize its obligation to develop such a program.

Organization of the Community College

Three essential factors condition the type of program needed in the thirteenth and fourteenth years and hence determine the major aspects of organization:

1. Since a large proportion of young people will be expected to continue their education through the thirteenth and fourteenth years, it should be possible for many of them to live at home, as they now do to attend high school. Hence there must be a large increase in the number of institutions serving essentially their local communities.
2. The senior high school and the first two years of college, particularly the liberal arts college, are similar in purpose, and there is much duplication of content in their courses. The program of the community college must dovetail closely therefore with the work of the senior high school.
3. In most states there are many communities of a size too small to warrant their maintaining community colleges. It is essential, therefore, that the community colleges—including technical institutes, university branches, and the like—be planned on a state-wide basis and administered in such a way as to avoid expensive duplication and to provide training for each vocation somewhere. Such training should be made available to qualified students regardless of their place of residence within the state.

The Special Role of the Junior College

In meeting these three major conditions, several problems of organization are involved. The first is the relation of the community college to the present junior college.

While the regular four-year colleges and universities include the thirteenth and fourteenth years of our educational system, the institution which has been developed especially to meet the needs of this age group is the institution now commonly called the "junior college." Its development has occurred almost wholly in the last 25 years.

The directory published in 1947 by the American Association of Junior Colleges shows that the enrollment in these institutions has grown from less than 51,000 in 1927–1928 to more than 400,000 in 1946–1947. The junior colleges listed number 648, including 12 located outside the continental United States and 14 which are lower divisions of four-year colleges. Of this total, 315 are publicly controlled, and 333 privately controlled. The publicly controlled ones, while fewer in number, enroll about 75 percent of the students. The average enrollment per junior college in 1945–1946 was public, 687, and private, 235, but there were still 140 public junior colleges enrolling fewer than 200 students each. As an indication of the extent to which the junior colleges serve the adults of their several communities, it may be noted that in 1944–1945 of the total enrollment about 65 percent were special students, generally adults, enrolled for the most part in evening classes.

The methods of control of the junior colleges vary. Sixty-three are controlled directly by a state or by a state institution; 180 by a local school district; 72 by a district organized especially for the control of the junior college; 191 by a religious denomination; 96 by a nonprofit board; 39 by a person or group who operate it as a proprietary institution; and 7 by other groups, chiefly the YMCA. As to length of curricula, 9 are one-year institutions; 599 are two-year institutions; 4 are three-year institutions; and 40 are four-year institutions, embracing generally the eleventh, twelfth, thirteenth, and fourteenth years. (All enrollment figures previously quoted include only the thirteenth and fourteenth years.)

It would appear from the above that the junior college is already making a significant contribution toward meeting the needs of those who wish to continue their education in their home communities beyond the high school. They are as varied in their programs as in their forms of control, and are flexible in their adjustment to local needs.

It is assumed, then, that the present junior college is pointing the way to an improved thirteenth and fourteenth-year program. A change of name is suggested because "junior" no longer covers one of the functions being performed. The name was adopted when the primary and often the sole function of the institution was to offer the first two years of a four-year college curriculum. Now, however, one of its primary functions is to serve the needs of students who will terminate their full-time college attendance by the end of the fourteenth year or sooner. For them a wide variety of terminal curricula has been developed. Such an institution is not well characterized by the name "junior" college. . . .

A careful study should be made in each state of the needs for more and better educational facilities at the thirteenth and fourteenth-year level. The State Department of Education, the public schools, the institutions of higher education both public and private, and interested laymen should join us in making the study in order that the resulting plan shall take into account the total educational resources as well as the total needs of the state. . . .

The Commission recommends that all states which have not already done so enact permissive legislation under which communities will be authorized to extend their public school systems through the fourteenth year. . . .

This Commission recommends that to serve this large group of small communities a statewide plan be developed embracing all communities large and small.

The Place of the Private and the Church-Related Community College

There are 96 privately controlled nonprofit junior colleges, 191 church-controlled, 39 proprietary, and 7 controlled by other organizations. Their enrollments in 1946–1947 totaled 78,150. Many of these junior colleges are the upper grades of schools with high school divisions and sometimes elementary schools as well.

The need for an improved and a more widespread opportunity for at least a two-year course beyond the high school is a challenge to church-related and other private colleges as much as it is to public institutions. It is quite possible, too, that some of the present four-year colleges will find it advantageous to stress even more than at present the work on the junior college level. Some may even discontinue their more expensive senior college work. This Commission recommends that both the junior colleges and the four-year colleges under private and church auspices have the fullest opportunity to be related to the movement to improve the program of the thirteenth and fourteenth years.

The last sections in volume 2 of the Truman Commission considers the relationship of the community college to colleges of arts and sciences, teachers colleges, universities, and professional schools and to proprietary schools.

The Commission placed the beginning of the junior college movement three decades prior—or later than the actual time—by a decade, or a century, or even several centuries, as will be seen in the next chapter:

> Until the junior-college movement began three decades ago, the four-year institutions and the proprietary schools provided practically all the educational facilities available beyond the high school. They still furnish the great bulk of instruction for the thirteenth and fourteenth years of our educational system. For every full-time student who entered a junior college or his first post-high-school year of college work in 1939–1940, there were four students who entered the regular universities and colleges. The colleges of arts and sciences, operating sometimes independently and sometimes as a part of a university, have carried the most of this instructional load at the junior-college level.

Finally, the Commission noted that education for the thirteenth and fourteenth grades would continue to be offered in four-year colleges and proprietary schools.

The last words of volume 2 cautioned about the dangers of "bigness": "The undergraduate and graduate enrollments of most public colleges are already far higher than their plant and facilities were designed to accommodate. We may not know the optimum size for colleges with different aims and programs. But that sheer bigness now threatens to lessen the effectiveness of education will undoubtedly be conceded by all familiar with the facts."

The report concludes, "This Commission believes that in the foreseeable future our nation will need more, separate, two-year and four-year college and university units of small size, located geographically in economical relation to population centers. These must be in addition to the recommended increase in community colleges."

CHAPTER 2

Origins of Two-Year Junior Colleges

At the time the Truman Commission on Higher Education was writing its report, which stressed the need for free, public, two-year community colleges to be established throughout the United States, there were about six hundred of such institutions already established. All were quite small.

In the United States the initial junior-college activity was in the private sector. In 1900, according to a table in "Analysis of Junior College Growth" in *Junior College Directory* (1961) by Edmund J. Gleazer Jr., there were only eight such organizations, all private. It is not likely that Dr. Gleazer included in his study two-year instruction in college subjects provided in seminaries and several church bodies, such as the Mormons.

Some religious bodies, for example the Society of Jesus (Jesuits), had been providing the equivalent of the first two years of a four-year college education to men entering the organization, with certain studies taken prior to those in philosophy and theology. By their coursework, these men were in direct preparation for the priesthood. In this country the first Jesuit course of this kind, called "the Juniorate," was offered in 1806 at Georgetown College a few miles from our nation's capital. In the early decades of the nineteenth century, Jesuit Juniorates were located in Frederick, Maryland, and Florissant, Missouri.

The Jesuit two-year Juniorates had been established in Europe all through the seventeenth and eighteenth centuries. It is likely that some of the founders of junior colleges in America in the early decades of the nineteenth century were aware of the classical studies of the two-year Juniorate in Jesuit seminaries and equivalent courses under other religious sponsorship.

The concept of a lower and upper division to the college level of higher education originates at the very beginning of such education in the western world. The medieval universities in Europe founded in the thirteenth, fourteenth, and fifteenth centuries had their basic studies in two divisions, the trivium and the quadrivium. The trivium embraced grammar, rhetoric, and logic. These subjects—all studied in Latin— were intended to develop in the student a firm command of spoken and written language, and at least an introduction to clear-thinking. The quadrivium covered arithmetic, music, geometry, and astronomy. In those times music was studied importantly for its relationship to mathematical concepts. Together the trivium and the quadrivium constituted the famed seven liberal arts of the medieval universities. Following this education, students went on to study philosophy and theology. The majority of such students—then only males—became clergymen. Likewise many of the graduates of the colonial colleges (established in what was to become the United States) became clergymen. Prior to the Civil War, only a handful of college presidents were laymen; the overwhelming majority were clergymen. It is interesting to note that with relatively few exceptions the junior colleges founded in the United States were under lay sponsorship.

Another facet in the development of the concepts that led to the Truman Commission in 1947 was the great success of two important actions by the nineteenth-century Congress: The Morrill Act of 1862 and the second Morrill Act of 1890. These acts made possible the so-called land-grant colleges, as the endowments were provided for from the sale of tens of thousands acres of federal land in western states.

James Morrill of Vermont sponsored both of these acts of Congress. The first act, passed during the middle of the Civil War and signed by President Abraham Lincoln, had a contemporary aspect, as states in rebellion against the Union were not eligible for land grants. In fact, they could not be eligible because the legislation based each state's land-grant acreage on the number of senators and members of the House of Representatives of that state. War conditions naturally made it impractical for any state to secure the land grant, sell the acreage for the endowment, and raise the other funds necessary for construction.

Wisely recognizing that the growth of the country and the beginnings of manufacturing called for large numbers of workers trained in scientific methods, Morrill asked for state-sponsored colleges that would train men and women in agricultural methods, mining, and the technology of the times, in addition to offering liberal arts for those who wanted courses in those areas. Every land-grant institution was required to offer military training. Until the opening of land-grant colleges after the Civil War, with few exceptions, all colleges were directed by clergymen and most all of them were under a religious denomination sponsorship. The small number of colonial colleges (established mostly by grants from the English Crown) and the several hundred denominational colleges (established from the end of the Revolutionary War to the Civil War) were only for males. Land-grant colleges—another forecast of the junior or community colleges of the next century—opened the way for large-scale higher education of women.

The second Morrill Act did not come until 1890, toward the end of the congressman's lengthy service in the U.S. Congress, and on the eve of the development of two-year colleges. This Morrill Act featured provisions for land-grant institutions serving African Americans in states that had barred education—at any level—to them.

William Rainey Harper, president of the University of Chicago at the turn of the twentieth century, introduced the concept of upper and lower divisions of the college. At this time universities were more interested in specialized academic and graduate studies, and faculties were less interested in students in their first two years of college. The University of Chicago awarded the first associate's degree (A.A.) in the United States.

If anyone deserves the title of father of the nonsectarian two-year or junior college in the United States, it is the Reverend Frank Gunsaulus. At the age of thrity-one he was pastor of the Plymouth Church in Chicago. One Sunday in 1890 he gave an impassioned address that became known as "The Million Dollar Sermon." In it he stressed the urgent need for a two-year post-high-school institution that would provide training in engineering, chemistry, architecture, and library science as well as courses in the liberal arts which could be transferred to a four-year college.

That sermon made a deep impression on Philip Danforth Armour of the wealthy meatpacking and grain-merchant family. Armour agreed to provide the million dollars, a tremendous sum at that time, on two conditions: that the Reverend Gunsaulus would head the institution, knowing that he would make up for his lack of experience in the world of education with his dedication and enthusiasm; and that the institution would bear the name of Armour.

In 1893, three years after the sermon, the Armour Institute opened its doors to students. It continued under that name until 1940 when it merged with the Lewis Institute (established in 1895) to form the still existing Illinois Institute of Technology.

Reverend Gunsaulus's slogan gives a measure of the man and suggests why the Armour Institute under his leadership was such a success: "Heads, hand, and heart trained to work in unison and you have an idea of what our school is struggling to accomplish." Frank Gunsaulus is perpetuated in the name of a Chicago high school.

Joliet Junior College in Joliet, Illinois, has been hailed as the first junior college under public auspices with a founding date of 1901. High-school authorities began in that year to provide two years of college work to the small number of their graduates who sought studies, primarily so that they could transfer to four-year colleges. Many years passed before the Joliet High School actually set up the Joliet Junior College with its own building and specific financing.

Lewis Institute in Chicago is generally regarded as the second of the private two-year junior colleges. Notwithstanding its name, the school provided technical and academic courses, transferable to the junior year of a four-year college.

Junior colleges were set up in small but increasing numbers in the early decades of the twentieth century. The founding reasons were diverse. In some cases a high school wanted to provide two years of college training to some of its graduates because of the economic and distance obstacles. In other cases a whole community or region felt the desire to provide a junior college to some of its high-school graduates for educational and civic reasons. A number of communities recognized the importance of having a junior college to help employers and to increase civic pride. Another reason for the establishment of post-high-school institutions was the growing importance of technology and science. The United States was shifting from a country essentially based on agriculture to one predominately grounded in manufacturing. This change led to the development of two-year technical schools. Some normal schools or teaching/training institutions took on the name of "community college." Another type of junior college was the so-called finishing school run by several orders of nuns in the United States.

At the turn of the century, according to *Junior College Directory* by C. C. Colvert and H. F. Bright (1952), there were only six junior colleges in existence, with two-thirds of them private, and of these two were situated in Chicago. Growth in the number of junior colleges was slow. By 1920, the year that the American Association of Junior Colleges was formed, there were eighty-seven junior colleges, of which more than half were private. Twenty years later, just before our entrance into World War II, the total number was close to three hundred, with privates still predominant. By the time the Truman Commission on Higher Education issued its report, the number of junior colleges under local or state sponsorship exceeded those under private control.

The number of students in public two-year institutions matched those in private ones by 1920, as the public institutions were much larger. By World War II, approximately three-quarters of these students were in public post–high schools, according to Edmund J. Gleazer's "Analysis of Junior College Growth" in the 1961 *Junior College Directory.*

A small number of faculty members at Teachers College, Columbia University, paid attention to the private junior colleges and those started under public school, district, or state auspices from the early years of the twentieth century. At that time the major interest in education beyond elementary school focused on the high school, a level of education that had become universal.

There were faculty and students at Teachers College who heeded the junior-college movement from its earliest days. Some encouraged the establishment of the American Association of Junior Colleges, formed in 1920 when many of the most influential institutions still were under private sponsorship. Teachers College was regularly represented at the AAJC annual conventions and faculty members closely followed the activities and problems facing two-year colleges.

An outstanding example of how Teachers College professors were able to provide critical assistance to the community-college movement in its early decades can be found in the work of Dr. George Drayton Strayer and his associates known as "the Strayer group." Significant help was furnished, enabling the city of Chicago to work out a junior-college system after a "founding period" that lasted twenty-three years.

The story is told in detail by Elbert K. Fretwell Jr., in his chapter "Success Built on Tragedy" in *Founding Public Junior Colleges* (1954). In the 1911–1912 school year, the Chicago Board of Education furnished college level courses to twenty students at the Crane Technical High School and twelve more at the Lane Technical High School. The following school year, Senn High School became the third in the group, with fifteen students, including some girls. In 1917–1918 the three programs were merged at Crane with four hundred students. The junior-college program continued to grow rapidly with over one thousand students by 1922–1923, when pressures were building for a plant of its own. Another program started at Medill High School of Commerce and Administration in 1919, which continued until June 1925. The Medill students joined those at Crane and the enrollment exceeded three thousand in 1926–1927.

Then misfortune hit the Chicago program. First there was a loss of accreditation in April 1930 for a variety of reasons. However, the accreditation was restored after one year. Students did not suffer; those who wished to transfer to four-year colleges were accepted because of the record made by earlier Crane graduates. The next setback came in June 1931 when the legal status of Crane was challenged. In December of that year, the Illinois Legislature gave the Chicago Board of Education authority to operate a junior college. The final difficulty was financial. The stock market crash of 1929 and the ensuing Great Depression hit Chicago very hard. The powerful *Chicago Tribune* led the campaign to end funding for Crane Junior College: "Any money which the Chicago Board of Education appropriated for a college is money taken from the children in the lower grades . . . under these circumstances it is idle to think of maintaining a free college."

The tide changed to public support for two main reasons: the work of "the Strayer survey group" from Teachers College, Columbia University, and the pressure from students and graduates of Crane. Dr. Strayer told a mass meeting on June 6, 1932, at Chicago's Auditorium Hotel, "The survey proposes without hesitation that the Crane Junior College is an essential part of your educational system and should be retained." The report suggested that "Chicago had only begun to take care of its post-high-school population." Noting that Chicago liked to compare itself with New York City, the report stressed that free higher education was provided in New York City, a point that rebuts the stand of those who felt Crane College was an extravagance. A final conclusion of the Strayer survey was that "Chicago should give its one existing junior college more complete and adequate financing."

In September Crane was allowed to open with tuition fees but on a curtailed budget. Following the assassination of Mayor Anton Cermak on February 15, 1933, Edward Kelly became the new mayor and was able to appoint members to control the Board of Education. In July the board voted to discontinue Crane Junior College and use the building for high-school purposes.

Robert M. Hutchins, president of the University of Chicago, led the outcry against this action. Some stopgap programs were developed. One was financed with federal funds through the Civil Works Education Service (CWES). Space was provided for junior-college courses by the University of Chicago and by the Lewis Institute on Chicago's West Side.

Citizen pressures mounted, and in March 1934, the Board of Education, reflecting the altered view of Mayor Kelly, authorized a Chicago junior-college system with three branches: South Side Junior College (later Woodrow Wilson), Wright Junior College on North Side, and Medill Junior College (later Herzl). Collectively these units comprised the Chicago City Junior College. The new junior-college units of Chicago opened on September 17, 1934.

CHAPTER 3

Teachers College and the Associate Nursing Degree

Within a year of the issuance of the Truman Commission's Report on Higher Education, those interested in nursing education realized that community colleges might provide the ideal site for the expansion in nursing needed by the projected population growth and the increased complexities of the field.

Discussions on the subject—which included the Nursing Department of Teachers College, Columbia University—resulted in a 1949 proposal by the National League for Nursing Education to the American Association of Junior Colleges (AAJC). This proposal suggested that these two organizations should form a committee to determine how already existing junior colleges and the many hundreds of two-year institutions (which were to be known as community colleges) could successfully develop effective programs leading to an associate's degree in nursing. The committee was motivated by education and a longstanding medical tradition.

In March 1950 the Joint Nursing Committee issued a report agreeing that the junior college was the logical place for the preparation of nurses and proposed the establishment of a national advisory committee of representatives of junior colleges and national nursing organizations. The person principally involved in carrying out the mandate of the Joint Committee was Mildred L. Montag, initially a doctoral candidate and then professor of nursing at Teachers College. She wrote a detailed study of nursing in the United States as it entered the post–World War II era and developed a comprehensive curriculum for a nursing course at two-year colleges.

Dr. Montag's dissertation was turned into a book, *The Education of Nursing Technicians*, published by John Wiley & Sons in 1951. Dr. R. Louise McManus, director of the division of Nursing Education at TC, wrote the foreword. The book was reprinted in 1971 as the first in the six-volume Wiley paperback nursing series.

It was recognized that a program in nursing in two-year colleges needed to be based on extensive research. The Joint Committee attempted to obtain a grant from one of the traditional sources of foundation support but was not successful. However, in 1952—the year after the Montag study was in print—Mrs. Nelson Rockefeller made a grant of $110,000 to the division of Nursing Education at TC based on a proposal prepared by Dr. R. Louise McManus using the data of Dr. Montag's dissertation. Mrs. Rockefeller's gift was anonymous but her name was disclosed in 1963 in Dr. Michael Brick's dissertation. The project was known as the Cooperative Research Project in Junior and Community College Education for Nursing, with Mildred Montag as the director. The project was funded for the years 1952 to 1956. The goal was to prepare "bedside nurses who could qualify for licensure as registered nurses and who could meet the institution's requirements for an associate degree," according to her Dr. Montag.

Both TC and the AAJC appointed members to an advisory committee that guided the project and explained the benefits of a nursing-degree program to two-year college administrators. Dr. Montag's assistant directors were knowledgeable about community junior colleges: Marion Buechel, former president of Everett Junior College, Washington (director for two years), Walter E. Sindlinger (director for two years), and Larry Gatkin (director for one year).

Dr. Montag cited the Truman Commission's Report on Higher Education to support her position that the professional education of nurses should be in degree-granting institutions. Historically the bulk of nursing education in the United States had been hospital-based. This education was essentially an apprentice type of on-the-job training with the participants spending long hours of their three-year course functioning as nurse's aides in hospitals.

Dr. Montag recognized that her proposed title of "nursing technician" would not likely become popular or "satisfy forever" but it suggested that the functions of a nurse could be conceived on a continuum, running from the practical through technical and on to professional.

Turning again to the Truman Commission report, Dr. Montag suggested that in the postwar world, it was estimated that there were five jobs requiring two years of preparation to every one needing four years of preparation. This substantiated the potential role of the two-year college in nursing education.

In order to develop the whole person, the following observation of the Truman Commission was cited: "If the semiprofessional curriculum is to accomplish its purpose, however, it must not be crowded with vocational courses to the exclusion of general education. It must aim at developing a combination of social understanding and technical competence. Semiprofessional education should mix a goodly amount of general education for personal development with technical education that is intensive, accurate, and comprehensive enough to give the student command of marketable abilities."

Stressing the need for a balance between technical and living skills, Dr. Montag wrote, "Traditionally, nursing education, whether for registered or practical nurses, has been almost exclusively technical. It is obvious that it is necessary for the individual to be able to adjust to the world in which she lives. Most programs for nursing technicians will be terminal programs and so they should provide four kinds of competency—occupational, social, civil, and personal. The complex society in which we now live requires that the individual have considerable understanding and the ability to cope with the problems encountered. Skill in the art of communications, knowledge of the economic system, understanding of people and social institutions, and an appreciation of the privileges and obligations of citizenship are all necessary if the student is to be able to function effectively as a person as well as a technician."

The first law governing the licensing of nurses was passed in North Carolina in 1903. At the time of Dr. Montag's book (1951), six states plus Hawaii and Puerto Rico had laws on this subject, but only in four—New York, Arkansas, Louisiana, and Hawaii—were the laws mandatory. Dr. Montag argued that for the public's protection, nurses-for-hire should have a license; hence it was clear that the program being advocated for junior community colleges would lead to a license in the particular state. "The prosposal made here is that there should be one licensure for nurses—one which sets the minimum which is required for the safety of the public."

The purpose of these proposed two-year programs in nursing was "to provide an educational program, for young women and men, which will prepare them to carry on certain of the techniques of nursing in the hospital and in the home, and to live effectively as persons and as citizens of the community."

The proposal suggested that the ideal institution to provide the education for the nursing technician was the community college. "The community college, as seen by the President's Commission, is recommended as the preferable institution because of its purpose, its location, and the variety of curricula it will offer. Until such a time as the community colleges grow and develop in sufficient number to meet the need, curricula for nursing technicians may be set up in junior colleges and technical institutes."

Addressing the cost—since the traditional nursing education had been free or nearly so—Dr. Montag again cited the Truman Commission: "Public education through the fourteenth year of schooling be made available, tuition free, to all Americans able and willing to receive it, regardless of race, creed, color, sex, or economic and social status." Up to this time, few persons of color were able to become trained nurses. There would continue to be a role for private institutions in nursing education but the needs of society must be met through the use of public funds.

Next Dr. Montag broached the problems of designing a nursing program for a two-year college. First she noted that there is no objective evidence to show the length of time required to acquire the skills and understanding needed in nursing. This was true because the traditional programs for registered nurses had been work-centered instead of student-growth-centered. The objective was an academic two-year program that should be "carefully planned and controlled." The hypothesis was that such a program would accomplish more than the three-year ones in which "the student literally pays her way by extra practice."

The proposed curriculum had two parts: General classes combined with courses "designed to prepare the student for social and personal competency." Courses in general education included those designed to develop facility in oral and written communication, an appreciation of the arts, basic psychology, and the role of the citizen. Coursework also included history, sociology, economics, and government. For such courses, the regular faculty of a community college, junior college, or technical institute would be available.

"The technical portion of the curriculum is essentially new since there is no program of this type currently offered," Dr. Montag stated. In her opinion, the aim in this area should be the development of the required skills to give nursing care to patients. These skills should be acquired in the environment in which they are to be practiced. Courses should include biology, microbiology, human growth and development, nutrition, and the nursing arts, including the needs of various age groups and types of illnesses. Science courses should have appropriate laboratory sessions. This part of the curriculum should emphasize the practical with actual experience in hospitals, clinics, and nursing homes. Her suggested curriculum:

FIRST YEAR	Credits		Credits
First Semester		*Second Semester*	
Communication Skills	3	Communication Skills	3
Human Biology	3	Human Growth and Development	3
General Sociology	3	Nutrition	2
Elementary Economics	3	Microbiology and Community Hygiene	2
Orientation to Nursing	4	Medical-Surgical Nursing	6
Physical Education	0	Physical Education	0
Total	16	Total	16

SECOND YEAR	Credits		Credits
First Semester		*Second Semester*	
Literature	2	Literature	2
History of the United States	3	Introduction to Government	3
Nursing of Children (including		Psychiatric Nursing	4
communicable diseases)	4	Medical-Surgical Specialties	
Nursing of Mothers and Infants	4	(including tuberculosis)	6
Mental Hygiene	3	Elective	2
Physical Education	0	Physical Education	0
Total	16	Total	17

The amount of time she suggested for the clinical portion of the curriculum was:

Orientation to Nursing	First Semester	2 hours class	6 hours clinical experience per week for 16 weeks
Medical-Surgical Nursing	Second Semester	3 hours class	9 hours clinical experience per week for 16 weeks
Nursing of Children	Third Semester	2 hours class	6 hours clinical experience per week for 8 weeks

Nursing of Mothers and Infants	Third Semester	2 hours class	6 hours clinical experience per week for 8 weeks
Psychiatric Nursing	Fourth Semester	2 hours class	6 hours clinical experience per week for 8 weeks
Nursing in Medical-Surgical Specialties	Fourth Semester	3 hours class	9 hours clinical experience per week for 8 weeks

Dr. Montag believed that this new type of nursing program, designed for two-year colleges, required specially trained administrators in order to be successful. The last part of her book is devoted to administrators for those nursing programs. She wrote, "The choice of key personnel who understand and accept the policies of the institution and are prepared to implement them is one of the most important functions of administration."

Nursing programs organized in junior community colleges were set up in already existing institutions. Dr. Montag noted that it may be assumed that such institutions will be sympathetic to the needs of the nursing administrators and their administrators. These administrators must be responsible for seeking well-qualified nursing faculty to teach nursing courses and also must be able to interpret the needs of the nursing students for the general education courses. Administrators of the nursing program should have a direct influence in the selection of students for that program.

A review of the curriculum offered at that time by Teachers College indicated that many of the existing courses would be appropriate for the training of faculty and administrators of the new two-year program in nursing. Dr. Montag suggested the addition of several courses: philosophy of the community college, psychology of the late adolescent and young adult, administration of programs for nursing technicians, financing nursing education and budget planning for nursing programs, teaching nursing to nursing technicians, and observation and practice teaching in programs for nursing technicians. Her reason for a course on the philosophy of the community college was explained in these words: "The increasing emphasis on the extension of the educational period for all youth makes it necessary to understand the institution offering education at this level. The terminal nature of programs of community colleges influences the philosophy and policies of the institutions. Understanding the purposes of community colleges should make it easier for faculty members to work within this framework."

In conclusion, Dr. Montag wrote, "The main purpose of this study has been to plan an educational program for the nurse with predominately technical functions and to propose a program for the preparation of professional nurse personnel for faculty in these programs." The study ended by stressing the need for experimentation in determining the most suitable program to train the professional nurse administrators as well as finding the best curriculum to train the nursing students in two years.

Dr. Walter E. Sindlinger, who closely followed the Cooperative Research Project in Junior and Community College Education for Nursing, summed up the development in 1995 this way: "Concerned about the lack of academic preparation typical RN's were receiving in hospital schools, Professor Montag had proposed a new and innovative curriculum which was designed to be used in community colleges. The purpose of the research project then was to test her idea—to see if community colleges could indeed develop programs, following the general guidelines she proposed, which would prepare nurses who could qualify for licensure as registered nurses and for the associate degree."

An indication of the tremendous success of the two-year nursing program was that by 1970, some six hundred community colleges were offering such a program, and by 1990, about eight hundred.

CHAPTER 4

How to Do It Guidelines

A most helpful assistant to individuals and groups interested in the establishment of a public community college in their area came out of Teachers College, Columbia University, in 1954 through Elbert K. Fretwell, Ph.D. That year, TC's Bureau of Publications issued a 142-page book titled *Founding Public Junior Colleges: Local Initiative in Six Communities*.

To support the guidelines that were printed in an appendix, the volume gave detailed histories of the founding of the six selected two-year institutions. The author studied two institutions in the Midwest: Joliet Junior College and Chicago City Junior College; two in California: San Bernadino Valley College and Contra Costa Junior College District; and two in the East: Montgomery Junior College in Maryland and Orange County Community College in New York State.

Dr. Fretwell set the stage for his presentation in his opening paragraph:

By 1970, the number of young people of college age in the United States will, it is estimated, be approximately double that of 1943. Even if the percentage of the college-age population now enrolled in some form of post-high-school education does not increase, this careful prediction, based on recent birth rate trends, has great significance for the youth of our country, for employers, for leaders in education and government, and for all other citizens.

Then a series of questions were asked: On the basis of physical space alone, what percentage (of students knocking at the doors of the colleges) can be admitted? What will be the effect on standards of instruction if provisions are not made to maintain the present level of teaching, let alone develop plans for its improvement? Should more rigid entrance requirements be established to keep the enrollment to that which present colleges can handle adequately? What effect would such a step have on preparation of the increased number of professional and semiprofessional workers needed by an enlarged population? In an age when gaining entrance to college will involve strenuous competition, what will happen to the young person of promising abilities but limited financial means? To one who aspires to a career in a profession but who lives far from existing institutions? To the slow-maturing but potentially valuable young person uncertain of his goals? Or to a student who seeks a shorter-than-four-year course to prepare him for his chosen vocation?

Elsewhere in his introductory chapter, Dr. Fretwell wrote: "The American junior college as we know it is essentially a product of the twentieth century. Although a few small private junior colleges now in operation [1954] trace their beginnings to the last century, the establishment of the first public junior college at Joliet, Illinois, in 1901 marks the start of an era of expansion and diversification. Precisely how many junior colleges have opened their doors since that date is unknown because an indeterminate number has gone out of existence. But by 1950–51, there were 577 junior colleges in operation in the United States; institutions of this type were functioning in the District of Columbia and in every state except Nevada and New Mexico. Their total enrollment at that time was approximately 575,000 students."

Dr. Fretwell continued, "Present-day junior colleges continue to prepare recent high-school graduates to enter the junior year of four-year college, but this is now only one of their major objectives. The modern junior college concerns itself also with vocational training for those who will seek employment after one or two years of study. It may place its major emphasis on general education for citizenship. Short-term and extension courses, and offerings for persons of all ages, receive significant attention in many junior colleges. Ideally, if a given organization is large enough, it can and should seek to become a comprehensive community college."

Byron S. Hollinshead's report for the Commission on Financing Higher Education (1952) recommending a community college in any population center over twenty thousand was quoted. The statement of James B. Conant, a former president of Harvard, endeavored to make two-year college courses "fashionable" and "to create a climate of opinion in which the length of the education beyond 18 is not considered the hallmark of its respectability."

Founding a junior college, it was pointed out, always involves dealing with a number of problems, some of which are difficult to solve. There usually is a significant time-lapse between the recognition of the need for a junior college in a particular area and the opening of such an institution to students. Dr. Fretwell called this "the founding period." His selection of six two-year colleges to study in detail intended to give underpinning to his guidelines, including a list of questions to be applied to a community considering the establishment of a local junior college. (See pages 30–31.)

Dr. Fretwell tried to give a representative sample in the six two-year colleges whose establishment was studied in detail. California already had a tradition of local, public junior colleges, and the state was in a position to provide financial and other assistance from the beginning for junior colleges planned in the 1950s. The two institutions in Illinois—Joliet and Chicago—were adding two years of college courses to high schools. The foundings in the Middle Atlantic States—Montgomery County, Maryland, and Orange County, New York—were chosen as examples in parts of the country where the junior-college movement was showing "signs of flowering."

While Dr. Fretwell expressed his belief that the detailed description of the individual founding periods may make known hitherto unavailable historical data, "a greater value of this book may be to provide information for students of the community college movement and for those considering establishment of a new college in their own locality."

On the basis of his case studies of the six junior colleges founded in several different areas of the United States, Dr. Fretwell devised a comprehensive checklist for those considering the establishment of such institutions. He felt confident that affirmative answers to all or most of the questions would assure—with reasonable certainty—success.

Checklist of Questions to Be Applied to a Community Considering Establishment of a Local Junior College

For the use of groups or individuals considering initiation of a junior college program, the author has prepared a checklist of questions to be applied to the community concerned. This list, which appears below, is intended as a starting point, not as a definitive outline or measuring instrument.

1. *Is there a distinct need for a junior college program?*
    a) Can the apparent need be identified in terms of the number of potential students and the services they will require?
    b) Can the interests, goals, aptitudes, backgrounds, and ages of the potential students be clearly studied and defined?
    c) Is a junior college program—defined in the broader community college sense—the best answer to the observed need?
2. *Does enabling or permissive legislation exist, or can it be brought into existence?*
    a) Is there positive state legislation providing for the legality of local junior colleges, or at least an absence of prohibitive legislation?
    b) Do existing state laws (if any) provide detailed instructions for junior college or junior college district organization?
    c) Do regulations specify what steps should be taken in order to qualify for state aid, where it exists?
    d) Should the possibility of sponsoring enabling legislation be considered?
3. *Are there individuals on the scene who can initiate necessary action?*
    a) Are there men or women in the area who possess qualities of insight and definite leadership?
    b) Are these people willing and able to work effectively with groups, and do they realize the challenges involved?
    c) If they are identified with special groups (labor, industry, or a particular profession, for example), can they understand the viewpoint of others?
    d) Will they be able to work with outside experts (from the state education department or a university) who may be invited to furnish appropriate assistance to the local organizing group?
4. *Is strong citizen support in evidence, or can it be developed and maintained?*
    a) Are the people of the area aware of the advantages of community college offerings?
    b) Are they willing to consider what other communities have done to develop locally sponsored higher education?
    c) Are they willing to work for organization of a college and not expect outsiders or paid professionals to handle *all* the details?

d) Would they go to the polls and vote to authorize and support a college, if such action were required?

e) Do they realize that a good instructional program costs money, and that usually over half of the outlay must be met by local sources?

5. *Can adequate financial support be assured?*

a) Can the district that the proposed college would serve support a good junior college program, assuming that citizens are in favor of such a program?

b) Are there provisions for state aid to locally organized junior colleges?

c) Can an equitable sharing of the cost be worked out between the local community, the state, and the students (where necessary)?

d) Can major cash expenditures be delayed (through use of temporary quarters or bond issues) without damage to the instructional program?

6. *Can space be secured and a teaching staff organized?*

a) Is it possible to obtain space for instruction, offices, and equipment in existing buildings on a temporary or permanent basis?

b) If not, will the college organization be in a position to acquire a definite site and erect its own plant?

c) Can a corps of instructors who are successful teachers in their respective fields and who are also in sympathy with the philosophy of the new college be engaged and retained?

d) If a large variety of instruction is to be offered (in vocational fields, for example), can qualified instructors be secured as needed on a part-time basis?

7. *Will students respond to the new educational opportunities?*

a) Is there a realization among potential students of the proposed junior college that there are advantages in attending the institution?

b) Will adults seize the opportunity to enroll as special students or to participate in evening, extension, or short-term courses?

c) Finally, can potential students afford to attend, both in terms of payment of tuition (if it must be charged) and in terms of time that would otherwise be devoted to remunerative employment?

If the answer to all or almost all of the questions listed above is YES for the community under consideration, it would appear, on the basis of the preceding six case studies, that success in founding a local junior college can be predicted with a reasonable amount of certainty.

CHAPTER 5

Ralph R. Fields

In 1948—just a year after the release of the Truman Commission's report calling for the establishment of comprehensive community colleges— Teachers College recruited to its faculty perhaps the most qualified person in this specialty in the country at that time: Ralph R. Fields.

From the earliest days of the junior college, TC was interested in the development of such institutions, sensing their future potential. TC faculty members consulted and advised junior-college administrators, and together they designed the appropriate higher-education administration and curriculum courses to serve the needs of those in the emerging field. This meant, for the most part, providing guidance to potential and enrolled TC students and directing them to suitable courses. Those courses were taught by well-prepared professors who were educated before the expansion of private two-year colleges where most students aimed at transferring to the junior year of a four-year college. After this expansion, the drive was for doubling the number of public two-year colleges and servicing a wide range of community educational needs.

Ralph R. Fields came from the West with broad knowledge of and professional experience in two-year postsecondary institutions. He was born in Arizona on April 29, 1907. After attending Phoenix Junior College, his first position in 1927–1928 was assistant registrar to that institution. In 1929 he received a B.A. degree from the University of Arizona. In 1931 he married Katherine J. Tinker.

After graduating from the University of Arizona, Fields taught for several years and was involved especially with curriculum matters at many Phoenix public schools. Fields moved his family—by then he and his wife had two children, Rodney and Kay Louise—from Arizona to California. This transfer made it possible for him to enroll in graduate education courses at Stanford University from which he received a master's degree and a doctorate in secondary education in 1940. The next year he was curriculum director of the San Jose, California, school system and then superintendent of schools.

The last position Dr. Fields held before moving from California to New York was at the California State Department of Education where he was primarily concerned with curriculum matters. During that period he became well acquainted with California's involvement in the community-college movement. Years later he wrote, "The state usually associated with the rapid spread of the movement is California. While not the first state to develop institutions known as junior colleges, California was among the first and has been the most prolific. The first major development in California was the passage by the state legislature in 1907 authorizing high schools to perform educational services which some were already performing. The law provided that the board of trustees of any city, district, union, joint union, or county high school could prescribe postgraduate courses of study for the graduates of its high schools or other high schools. The courses of study were to approximate the studies prescribed in the first two years of university courses. This, commonly recognized as the first legislation dealing with the infant junior college, was merely permissive. No support was offered to districts undertaking such service, only legal sanction."

Dr. Fields was also aware that California was the first state to see "the junior college as a dual-purpose institution, not simply a duplicate of the first two years of the university." This understanding of the junior college's role influenced all of Dr. Fields' work at Teachers College, Columbia University.

When Dr. Fields came to TC in 1948, he was placed in the Division of Instruction and soon became involved in various courses devoted to community colleges. In 1954–1955, he taught the first course with the title "The Community College" at TC. This basic course is still in the curriculum. His more specialized courses focused on teaching in community colleges and on research for various problems affecting those institutions. In 1958 he was among those who welcomed Walter E. Sindlinger to the TC faculty. Years before he had been a sponsor of Sindlinger's doctoral dissertation. Fields worked with Sindlinger on the grant application that resulted in the establishment at TC of the Community College Center, which was funded by the Kellogg Foundation in 1960. At that time he was teaching the basic community-college course jointly with Sindlinger. The next school year, 1961–1962, TC offered professional diplomas to executives of community or junior colleges.

Three years after Dr. Fields joined the TC faculty, President William F. Russell took steps to widen Fields's considerable expertise in the community-college field. President Russell believed that TC could make the greatest impact when carrying out the mandate of the Truman Commission by encouraging the development of public community colleges everywhere in the country.

There was little unknown by Dr. Fields and his fellow members of the Education Department at TC about the needs and opportunities for community colleges in the United States. But there was one concern: Was there knowledge to be acquired on the basis of the new postsecondary institutions in Great Britain?

On November 13, 1951, President Russell made a proposal to Dr. Fields, which he accepted two days later. Their letters follow.

**TEACHERS COLLEGE
COLUMBIA UNIVERSITY
NEW YORK 27, N.Y.**

OFFICE OF THE PRESIDENT

13, November 1951

Dear Ralph:

The Dean and I have been discussing the future of the Junior College in American education and the necessary planning for Teachers College and consequent program development. It seems probably that great expansion will take place in this area, somewhat comparable to that of the high school during the half-century past.

We both think that it would be very important to us, if we had more information available regarding parallel movements abroad, especially in Great Britain and possibly in Denmark and Switzerland.

Dean Caswell would like to send you on a special mission abroad, to take approximately six weeks, in order that you might study the foreign situation, talk with leaders and personally assess progress and results.

We propose to make you a grant toward your expenses of $2,000.00 and expense accounts up to this figure will be cared for by the College. As your plans mature, if it should appear that this sum is inadequate fully to care for your expenses, or for such materials as you might need to purchase, you can count on additional appropriation.

Faithfully yours,

(Signed by William F. Russell)

Professor Ralph Fields
Teachers College

TEACHERS COLLEGE
COLUMBIA UNIVERSITY
NEW YORK 27, N.Y.

DIVISION OF INSTRUCTION
OFFICE OF THE DIRECTOR

November 15, 1951

Dear President Russell:

I have your letter of November 13, containing your proposal that I study the equivalent of our junior college
and community college movement in Europe.

The prospect of becoming acquainted firsthand with the
budding county college movement in England and Wales, and
the junior college movement in Scotland, as well as the
more firmly entrenched technical colleges in Great Britain
and elsewhere, challenges me very much indeed. While it
will take some arranging of my spring program, I believe
it would be possible for me to free myself during late
spring for such a study.

This arrangement you suggest for expenses would be very
satisfactory and I will confer with you very soon to get
your further suggestions.

Sincerely,

(Signed by Ralph R. Fields)

President William F. Russell
Teachers College

In his book on the community-college movement (published by the
Bureau of Publications of Teachers College), Dr. Fields stresses the importance of the Truman Commission's report and its appeal that the
community colleges be comprehensive:

In 1947 the President's Commission on Higher Education brought the concept of the community college to the front pages of U.S. newspapers as well as to the attention of many educators who, prior to that time, had not given much serious thought to junior colleges. In its report the Commission clearly presents a definition of an emerging institution. It is fitting to observe one of several descriptions that the Commission included in its report.

Whatever form the community college takes, its purpose is educational service to the entire community, and this purpose requires of it a variety of functions and programs. It will provide college education for the youth of the community certainly, so as to remove geographic and economic barriers to educational opportunity and discover and develop individual talents at low cost and easy access. But in addition, the community college will serve as an active center of adult education. It will attempt to meet the total post-high-school needs of its community.

Dr. Fields points out that a public community college, following the appeal of the Truman Commission, should have five main characteristics. It should be 1) democratic, 2) comprehensive, 3) community-centered, 4) dedicated to lifelong learning, and 5) adaptable. He summarized: "To conclude, community colleges are like other colleges in some respects; we find in them many of the courses typical of all lower-division offerings and we find the usual semester of quarter hours of credit, admission requirements for certain curricula, and the like. But there are real differences. The range of occupational offerings is wider than typical and includes many callings not offered in the vocational work of most four-year colleges. Admission requirements are flexible, and the heterogeneity of students is marked. These differences are all indications of the efforts community colleges are making to adapt to the problems posed, the students enrolled, and the communities served."

In 1960 Dr. Fields was named associate dean of Teachers College. That same year he received the Distinguished Service Award of the New York State Association of Junior Colleges. The award was made at the organization's meeting held that year at the Orange County Community College. This is the institution where Dr. Sindlinger served as the first dean.

In 1961–1963 Dr. Fields traveled to Africa as the chief of party in the Teachers College project to train teachers in East African countries. This project was sponsored by the U.S. federal government. His book, *The Community College Movement*, was published by McGraw-Hill in 1962 as a part of its series in education. On his return from Africa, Dr. Fields resumed his teaching, mostly to graduate students interested in the community-college field.

Throughout his career, Dr. Fields stressed diversity and flexibility in community colleges. This is his viewpoint, in his own words: "because of the very nature of the movement, no two community colleges can be exactly alike. Each college is a reflection of the community served, the purposes sought, the functions undertaken, and the resources at hand."

A particular concern of Dr. Fields, from the time he first began teaching through his years as an education professor at TC and on into his retirement, was the curriculum in community colleges. He did not believe that a community college should add courses to suit all needs or wishes, but he did believe that the curriculum design in a community college posed problems that should be addressed by the faculty and administration of all community colleges. Dr. Fields believed that curriculum design should be approached from four angles: first, the relationship between designing courses and other phases of college life; second, the factors that influence the way in which courses are designed; third, the major methods of organizing courses and their advantages and disadvantages; and finally, the problem of planning for appropriate teaching procedures and learning activities.

"In the planning of courses in community colleges," he wrote, "we must constantly remind ourselves that this is a multipurpose institution. We must bear in mind, for instance, that important as the function of preparing students for further college work is, it is not the only one which the two-year college must implement. There is also the preparation of many individuals for appropriate vocational careers. There is also the general purpose of helping individuals to develop personally in relationship to their lives as homemakers, citizens, and people. Although certain courses will be planned to give major emphasis to one or another of these several purposes, nonetheless in each course some contribution to all is possible, if opportunities are seized."

Dr. Fields stressed the principles of learning as generally understood: "First, all behavior is learned and, therefore, all learning must be related to behavior, including intellectual behavior. Second, behavior is purposeful, and consequently all learning is purposeful. Third is that learning is discovery by the learner of a successful way of meeting a problem; and fourth, the learner usually must learn many things at the same time. Purposeful and meaningful learning is highly permanent."

Dr. Fields died at the age of ninety-three on November 15, 2000, in Sun City Center, Florida. His long life and dedication to education in a number of areas continues to be an inspiration to his successors at TC, in community colleges, and in higher education.

CHAPTER 6

Walter E. Sindlinger

For more than four decades, Walter E. Sindlinger was "Mr. Community College" at Teachers College. Beginning in 1938 in the M.A. program, he received a full-time faculty appointment in 1958. For many years he was head of the Community College Center and then—again for many years—he was chairman of the Department of Higher and Adult Education. Although he retired at the end of 1979, he continued to advise doctoral students and serve on dissertation committees until shortly before his death in 1995. After his retirement he was professor emeritus of the Higher Education Department. At Dr. Sindlinger's funeral service, his daughter, Judy, commented, "For years my sister and I thought the meaning of the word *vacation* was to visit community colleges."

Walter E. Sindlinger was born on February 14, 1914, in Gnadhutten, Ohio. His father was a high-school teacher and became the superintendent of schools. His mother was also a schoolteacher. Walter had polio, which left him with sensitivity in one leg. In the early days of the draft, this disease declared him unfit for military duty. However, after he was married in 1941, he was inducted and sent to Officer Candidate School. He spent much of his wartime service in the Armed Forces Institute as chief of the Division of Accreditation at the University of Rome. Complete educational services were provided. He was overseas when the first of his two daughters was born.

Sindlinger's first teaching position was as an English instructor in Pickerington and Galion high schools in Ohio. He was also involved in guidance at both institutions, an activity that forecast his deep involvement with students during his long tenure at TC. Not surprising, he was a graduate of Ohio University, receiving the A.B. degree in 1936.

In 1946, after his military service, he worked briefly in Princeton, New Jersey, for Audience Research, Inc., a Dr. George Gallup organization, whose clients included major motion-picture producing companies. For several years afterward, he was associated with an older brother, Alfred, in radio and television research based in Philadelphia. During much of this time, Sindlinger continued to take courses at Teachers College in New York City.

Moving to Middletown, New York, in 1950, Sindlinger began teaching at the Orange County Community College as an English instructor and a guidance counselor. Soon he was made dean. He took a leave of absence in 1952–1953 to concentrate on his work at TC.

In 1952 Sindlinger obtained two appointments at TC. The first was a part-time instructor position in curriculum and teaching, and the other was a research associate job. As a researcher, he had the opportunity to conduct detailed explorations of the operations of community colleges. His research was for the TC Nursing Department in connection with a joint project to develop a model of nursing education in community colleges. The research project resulted in his selection of a dissertation: *Guides to Experimentation in Education for Nursing in Junior and Community Colleges*. Mildred Montag, Margaret Lindsey, and Ralph R. Fields were members of that dissertation committee.

Commenting on his time at Orange County Community College, Sindlinger wrote, "I have especially enjoyed my work in the area of curriculum and teaching. I believe that a community college can and should provide opportunities for students of all ages and with a variety of personal educational needs. I also believe that these aims can best be accomplished by working closely with the students, the faculty, and the community through lay advisory committees. I like the challenge of problems, and I enjoy working to solve these problems, or to create new ideas."

More of Sindlinger's educational philosophy was articulated in his remarks at the dedication of a new building at the Orange County Community College in October 1955: "To those of us charged with the responsibility of administration and teaching, we seek guidance that our jobs may be well done. To those of us who are students, we seek guidance that our education may be concerned with more than knowledge and the learning of skills. We must also be concerned with our moral and spiritual life. We must also develop a good and sound philosophy of life. To those of use who are parents, we seek guidance that we may provide the heritage our children need. To all of us, we seek guidance so that our lives may be full and satisfying. That we continue to strive to uphold the Great Commandments and that through these efforts we may all move closer to a world of peace, freedom, and love for one another."

With his work on the Doctor of Education degree completed at Teachers College, Dr. Sindlinger accepted a position on the higher-education faculty of the University of Michigan, resigning his position as dean of the Orange County Community College, effective October 1, 1956. In announcing Dr. Sindlinger's departure, Edwin H. Miner, president of Orange Community College, expressed the following: "It is impossible to overstate the important role Walter Sindlinger has played in the development of the college from its struggling beginning six years ago. Under his capable supervision, the college staff has grown in size, stature, and efficiency. Other colleges and universities are accepting our recommended graduates as transfers with the full assurance that their academic preparation at Orange County Community College is both broad and thorough."

During their residency in Middletown, New York, the Sindlingers made an impact on the whole community. Dr. Sindlinger's wife, Agnes, taught at the Liberty Street School, which was also the school attended by their two daughters. The parents were active in the St. Paul's Methodist Church.

In June of that year, Dr. Algo D. Henderson, a well-known professor of higher education at the University of Michigan, Ann Arbor, wrote Walter Sindlinger, inviting him to consider applying to a new position in community-college education. The position involved both field services for the sixteen two-year colleges in the state—with several more planned—and teaching related to junior and community colleges. The job requirements included the following description: "His personality should be of the outgoing type, and effective in making personal contact. His academic competence should be sufficient to win the confidence of graduate students. Some experience as a dean would be desirable."

Dr. Sindlinger was ideally qualified for the Michigan University position and it is no surprise that he was appointed. His activities during the decade following the end of World War II demonstrate his zeal, enterprise, and enthusiasm. Few would have attempted such employment, much less succeed so well in it, especially with the crowded schedule of a dean of a community college, an instructor, a researcher, and a graduate student taking a large number of courses and writing a pioneering dissertation. Asa B. Elliott, vice president, G. P. Putnam's Sons, wrote, "I wish to offer congratulations on a fine piece of work which appears to be both interesting and informative to educators in nursing as well as the junior colleges."

Dr. Sindlinger sent an exhausting list of comprehensive annual reports to Algo D. Henderson, department chairman. They certainly are a prelude to his tireless work beginning in 1959 at Teachers College. In his two years in Michigan, he traveled widely for community-college visitation and conferences on planning new institutions. At the University of Michigan, he met on community-college matters with officials, administrators, and faculty, taught community-college and other higher-education subjects, and advised graduate students.

In an address to the annual Parent Education Institute in Ann Arbor, Dr. Sindlinger remarked that the discovery and development of every individual's talents at an early age will become more important as the nation's education system becomes more diverse. "Parents are going to have to recognize the values of other types of work besides white-collar jobs. Education beyond high school will reflect a multiple system of values."

In the spring of 1958, Dr. Sindlinger received an invitation to join the Teachers College faculty. He wrote to Dean Stephen M. Corey on April 19, 1958, "I look forward with eagerness to the beginning of my association with you and my many friends at Teachers College." Little did he know that the association would last for decades. The summer of 1958 was somewhat stressful as Dr. Karl W. Bigelow of TC urged Dr. Sindlinger to return to New York in time to teach in the summer session. The University of Michigan was sorry to lose him and wanted him to stay through the summer. The Sindlinger family moved to a new home constructed in New City, New York, in time for the fall TC classes. He moved from assistant professor rank at the University of Michigan to an associate professor at TC. At that time, higher-education courses, including those on community colleges, were in the Division of Administration and Guidance with Dr. John J. Norton, director.

Since Dr. Sindlinger had spent so much time at TC in the previous decade as a student, researcher, and instructor, it is not surprising that his appointment was greeted with enthusiasm by the education faculty. Typical was a letter from Dr. Willard S. Elsbree: "I am confident that you are aware that we were anxious for you to accept the offer, and you can count on our giving you support as you take up your new duties. We are all certain that this field is greatly in need of expansion and your coming will provide the needed stimulus." Ralph R. Fields, director of the Division of Instruction, with whom Dr. Sindlinger had had much contact as a graduate student, was very helpful in the relocation.

In September John Dale Russell, director of the Office of Institutional Research, wrote to Sindlinger, "It is certainly a grand achievement for Teachers College to have brought you back East again." Dr. Sindlinger was only at TC a short while when Dean Corey gave him the first of the many special assignments he was to have in increasing numbers over the years. Sindlinger was named to a TC committee that was planning a "Conference on Higher Education" for the spring of 1959. Elbert K. Fretwell Jr., assistant commissioner for Higher Education in The New York State Education Department and former TC faculty member, wrote, "It makes me feel terribly good that you are occupying 214A [Fretwell's former office at TC]. Please accept this as a compliment in the largest sense!"

An important date in TC's long involvement with community colleges was March 4, 1960. This date marked the opening of TC's Center for the Training of Administrators for Community and Junior Colleges with director Professor Walter E. Sindlinger, a member of the Department of Educational Administration.

Teachers College President Hollis Caswell announced the opening of the Community College Center—and its founding grant of $220,153 from the W. K. Kellogg Foundation—in the spring 1960 issue of *TC Topics* (vol. 9, no. 3). "The purpose of the Center is to help increase the supply of young administrators for the nation's community and junior colleges. The Center will plan a program to identify and recruit promising talent for the regular TC doctoral program in a community and junior college administration." Dr. John H. Fischer, dean of TC, commented, "If the development of the community college movement is to be a strong, healthful growth, much will depend on the leadership of these institutions. Teachers College welcomes the opportunity to help provide this leadership."

The program at TC Center offered students internships for educational, research, and consultant opportunities. This activity was facilitated by an advisory committee drawn from administrators of community and junior colleges in the New England and Middle Atlantic regions.

An announcement in *TC Topics* included a two-column photograph of the Charles Stewart Mott Center of Science and Applied Arts, a unit of the Flint (Michigan) Junior College, described as an outstanding example of an institution for which the new TC Center would prepare administrators. It was also noted that the dean at Flint Junior College, Dr. Clyde E. Blocker, was a TC graduate.

Dr. Sindlinger played a major role in Teachers College's grant application to the Kellogg Foundation and in designing the work of the Community College Center. John H. Fischer, TC dean, wrote to Dr. Ralph Fields on February 19, 1960: "When I read the proposal on the junior college administration program that you submitted to the Kellogg Foundation, I could well understand Maurice Seay's prompt and positive reaction to it. This is the best proposal to a foundation I have ever read. In what seemed to me exactly the right proportions, you have combined background information, general purposes, and specific operating arrangement. I am particularly impressed with the clear presentation of the total budget, which could not have been prepared so well had it not been preceded by very clear thinking about the program itself. I'm glad Maurice Seay was impressed too. Congratulations." Dr. Fields passed on Dean Fischer's memo with his own words to Dr. Sindlinger, "Add my kudos also. I've told John you did the bulk of the work."

The next year Dean Fischer wrote to Walter Sindlinger at some length: "I am enormously pleased with the progress you have been making. There is no doubt in my mind that under your direction our program will make a real difference in the junior college field. This is one project that should keep going after the Foundation funds are withdrawn because you are clearly laying foundations that will have permanent value. I like, too, the way you are setting up activities that can readily become a regular part of the college program."

One of the activities of the Community College Center was the selection of Kellogg Scholars who would receive tuition grants from among the students interested in two-year colleges. Other activities of the center included research in the variety of issues affecting those colleges that were growing in number at a very rapid rate.

Also that year, James E. Allen Jr., president of the University of the State of New York and commissioner of Education, appointed Dr. Sindlinger as a Teachers College member of the small Coordinating Council for the New York State Associate Degree Nursing Project.

Following a presentation and discussion period at the 1961 conference of the New York State Association of Deans and Guidance Personnel, Frank Chambers, dean of Broome Technical Community College, wrote, "Several of my colleagues of the two-year colleges expressed their pleasure at your excellent presentation. They felt that the discussion which followed was very stimulating and that you were the person with insight to student-personnel work in the community colleges."

In 1963 Dr. Sindlinger was promoted to full professor and given a trustee's appointment. That same year he became an authorized sponsor of Ph.D. dissertations at Teachers College. He was also appointed to the Ed.D. Committee and to the Faculty Executive Committee.

Yearly, or even more frequently, Dr. Sindlinger delivered a major address at an educational conference. Usually his topic was a new concern in the community-college field. For example, in 1967 he was chairman of the National Conference on Higher Education's discussion of "Unique Problems of Junior Colleges" in Chicago, sponsored by the Association for Higher Education. The next year he was the keynote speaker of the California Junior College Association's spring conference. This was a critical time as the California junior colleges were then authorized to function under their own Board of Governors, independently from the Board of the Colleges and Universities.

In the spring of 1968, Dr. Sindlinger was named chairman of Teachers College's Department of Higher Education. This meant he had to turn over the directorship of the Center for the Study of Community Colleges to Professor Michael Brick. While these responsibilities gave him much less time to study and teach about community colleges, he continued his abiding interest in that field until his death.

In 1969 Dr. Sindlinger received an offer to become a national consultant on community colleges. He graciously turned down the offer as he had with a number of proposals—he did not want to become president of a community college in another part of the country. In the words of the song, "His heart belongs to Teachers College."

Since Teachers College's outreach is international, over the years Dr. Sindlinger had many opportunities to meet with foreign visitors, many of whom sought information about how the benefits of community colleges might be achieved in their own countries. Most of the foreign students in the Department of Higher Education took courses in the community-college field as well as those concerned with four-year institutions and universities. In 1971 Gregorio C. Borlaza wrote about his appointment as president of the Philippine Normal College, which was the first institution of higher learning established by the United States in 1901. His letter explains how studies at TC in 1961 "helped very much in preparing me for my new position and for the other functions which have been assigned to me outside the college as chairman of the Teacher Education Committee of the Board of National Education, the highest educational-policy-determining body in this country."

During this period, Dr. Sindlinger also became a member of the Board of Counselors of Marymount College in Tarrytown. Marymount is a four-year liberal arts college for women, supervised by the Sacred Heart of Mary.

On the death of Professor Brick in 1974, Dr. Sindlinger again became director of the Center for Community and Junior College Administration. This was in addition to his post as chairman of the Department of Higher and Adult Education. At this time, he conducted a survey of graduates in community colleges and found there were twenty-five presidents and numerous deans and other administrators who had studied in the TC program. A number of these scholars had been Teachers College Kellogg Fellows.

In the fall of 1978, as Dr. Sindlinger was preparing to move to an emeritus professor status, Harold J. Noah wrote, "On behalf of deans and directors, I want to express my thanks to you for your thoughtful presentation of the case for the positions in the Department. Documents such as ours will, I am sure, help us towards recommendations that add up to better decisions for the college as a whole."

The January 1979 issue of *TC Advocate* was devoted to a celebration of Walter Sindlinger's long career at Teachers College. A page-wide banner headline read: "Simple Credo of a Great Professor: A Teacher Helps Others to Learn." Jerry Miller, a member of the publication's editorial board, wrote the story of his exclusive interview with Dr. Sindlinger on his retirement.

> With a twinkle in his eye, he fondly recalls his student days at TC and the warmth and concern of his doctoral mentor, Professor Ralph Fields, undoubtedly a model in his own professional development. There was a greater sense of community — a closeness between student and faculty that apparently has since dissipated. Those were the days when the president, dean, chairman, and faculty invited each other and their students into their homes. Education was not restricted to the classroom. . . .
>
> The man who is regarded as a pioneer in the junior community college movement in America reminds a visitor that today the "publish or perish" trap is stronger than ever. Prioritizing, the young teacher must devote most of his time and energies to research and publication — the art of teaching is superseded by the necessity to survive in a world of academic retrenchment. We need a new system of rewards. Not money but a merit system. Excellent teaching must be encouraged, recognized, and supported.

Dr. Sindlinger was noted as confident "that the community college is steadily moving towards the model of a 'public college,' serving all the real needs of a community and assisting in its redevelopment and survival."

That issue of *TC Advocate* includes a number of letters about Walter Sindlinger from his colleagues. The tone was set by the letter of Dr. John Fischer, former TC president: "Your contributions not only to TC but to the development of the community college as a powerful element in American education have earned you the well-deserved admiration of a large and grateful company." Dr. Lawrence Cremin, TC president at the time, wrote, "You have opened up a new field of study—junior college administration—and you have made the TC program a model for other institutions throughout the country."

The editorial in that issue of the TC Advocate had the heading: "A *Mensch* in Academe" and included the following statement: "In the role of professor as scholar, he has tirelessly guided hundreds of neophytes in the search for truth, grounded in ethics and integrity. In the role of professor as artist, he has been a virtuoso in the classroom. He is, indeed, a teacher of teachers. In the role of professor as person, he has been a model in manifesting the humanistic virtues of understanding, sincerity, and compassion."

Following his formal retirement, Walter Sindlinger continued to advise graduate students, served on dissertation committees, and worked as a consultant in the field of higher education. Not very long before his death, he prepared a brilliant TC seminar paper on the history of TC's involvement with community colleges. This book owes a great debt to that paper. The seminar took place on April 27, 1995, a month and a half prior to his death.

CHAPTER 7

Michael Brick

With quite a different background than Ralph R. Fields, Walter E. Sindlinger, or his other colleagues involved in community-college matters
at Teachers College, Michael Brick was in a position to add a new and
important perspective. He did not come out of the Midwest or the West
from a small-town background. He was a big-city boy, born and educated in Brooklyn, New York. He grew up keenly aware of the problems of the economically depressed and of those discriminated against
for a variety of reasons.

Born on March 27, 1922, he received his formative education in
the New York City public schools. He received his A.B. degree with
majors in history and political science in 1941 from Brooklyn College
of the University of the City of New York (CUNY). In those days,
CUNY higher education was free to qualified students and was the
path of upward mobility for thousands of New Yorkers. From 1943
until 1946, the year after the end of hostilities in World War II, Mike
Brick was in the United States Army.

From 1946 to 1949 he was a journalist with the *Mirror*, a daily news-
paper in New York City. Unquestionably, the years in journalism gave
Mike a perspective on the educational needs of the "common man," not
common to many in teaching.

Mike Brick then turned to public relations, another unusual career
background in the development of future educators. He served from
1950 to 1952 as public relations director of Bradstreet Fashions.
Throughout those years, he was also a part-time student at Teachers
College, receiving an M.A. in history in 1950. In 1952 he began his

professional-education career at Orange County Community Teaching College. In 1954 he was made chairman of the Social Sciences Department. From 1958 to 1960 he was the dean of the Dutchess Community College in nearby Poughkeepsie, New York.

With his longtime interest in history and his years of teaching it to community-college students, Mike Brick decided that his own dissertation in American history would be impeccable. His subject was the story of the origin, development, and influences of the American Association of Junior Colleges (now the American Association of Community Junior Colleges). He decided to be a candidate for the Ph.D. in history rather than the more usual Ed.D. at Teachers College. The Ph.D. in history involved the participation of the Columbia University's history department in coursework and faculty representation on the dissertation committee. In 1963 Dr. Brick received the Ph.D. degree of which he was very proud, believing that it reflected well on the whole community-college field. His book, *Forum and Focus for the Junior College Movement—The American Association of Junior Colleges*, based on his dissertation, was published by the Bureau of Publications of Teachers College.

The News Office of TC chose to feature the concern expressed by Dr. Brick in his book on a trend in the early 1960s that demanded stricter admission requirements in junior colleges. The press release stated:

> If continued, the trend could lead to the deprivation of the only post-high-school education available to many qualified people in a community and to the loss of manpower and special occupational skills that these institutions are intended to provide to the communities in which they are located.
>
> Dr. Brick reports that a growing number of junior colleges are adopting the often highly selective and often 'undemocratic' admission policies of the four-year liberal arts colleges. This approach could leave the newer institutions junior colleges in name only, without the vitality and direct responsiveness to the needs of the society for which they were created. The commitment of the American people to equality of educational opportunity is as strong as ever.

The alarm sounded by Dr. Brick was certainly heard as junior colleges increasingly called themselves community colleges—following the Truman Commission's lead—and became more comprehensive.

Traditional admission standards continued to be required for students hoping to transfer to four-year institutions. For other programs, admission requirements were minimal or nonexistent.

Dr. Brick was concerned that some administrators and trustees of junior colleges could "hardly wait" to turn their institutions into four-year colleges. That trend did not last. During the 1960s there was a heightened recognition of the community college's permanence in American education.

For two-year colleges, both those existing at the time and the large number of planned colleges, Dr. Brick listed the following objectives in his book:

1. Special attention to technical education and community service. A great challenge to education, one that must be met by junior colleges, is automation. "Today's skills may become obsolete overnight, and new skills not yet visible may be required overnight," he states. Dr. Brick maintains that "technical training, interwoven with general education, is, and ought to be, a major concern of the two-year colleges. The need is overwhelming in this country and abroad for personnel trained at this level."

2. State legislation that allows "freedom of action to junior colleges and removes politics, as far as possible, from education." The junior college "must have independence."

3. State and, if necessary, federal financial support of junior colleges. Substantial money must come from these sources if colleges "are to be within the financial reach of prospective students."

4. A higher level of professional competence of junior-college administrators and teachers. Strong junior-college teacher-preparation programs and inservice workshops and institutes must be established.

Forum and Focus for the Junior College Movement contains an appendix saluting the thirty-four educators—the majority being junior-college administrators—who met in St. Louis on June 30 and July 1, 1920, for a national conference of junior colleges. The conference established the American Association of Junior Colleges. George F. Zook, then a specialist in higher education at the U.S. Bureau of Education, attended the meeting. In 1946 he was selected by Harry Truman to be chairman of the President's Commission on Higher Education.

Professor Brick joined the faculty of Teachers College in 1960 as an instructor. He rapidly rose the academic ladder, becoming assistant professor in 1963, associate professor and director of the Community College Center in 1965, and professor and chairman of the Department of Higher and Adult Education in 1971. Over the years his consulting work in the community-college field increased until he became one of the best consultants in the country.

Michael Brick was a tireless worker in his roles as a researcher, administrator, or teacher. He was a forceful and persuasive speaker. In the classroom, his aggressive style aimed at constantly challenging his students to understand all the facets of a question as well as he did. He would probe until he was satisfied that everyone in his class or seminar had a full knowledge of the matter under discussion. Outside the classroom, he was helpful to his students and others who sought his guidance.

Alongside his teaching, administering, and consulting, Dr. Brick found time to do a good deal of writing. The October 1967 issue of *Junior College Journal* published his article "Two Plus Two," an analysis of how certain technology programs in high schools and in two-year colleges of New York State sought ways to initiate articulation procedures. This article was based on data assembled for the benefit of a work conference held at the Greystone Conference Center in Riverdale, New York, in October 1966. According to Dr. Brick, the research found that "there is a good deal of misunderstanding among high schools in regard to the work of the two-year colleges and among community colleges in what high schools are attempting to do in vocational-technical education. In many instances there is wasteful duplication of effort as well as poor counseling on both levels as a result of lack of proper information." His final point was the question: "What immediate activities can be undertaken to improve articulation between high schools and community colleges in the areas of technical education?"

In 1966 Dr. Brick was a key member of the Task Force on Higher Education in Washington, D.C. That report made recommendations for the implementation of the federal law passed on November 7, 1966, to turn the Federal City College and Washington Technical Institute into a comprehensive community college serving the educational needs of the many citizens in our nation's capital. One of the research assistants on the project was Dr. Joseph N. Hankin, then a recent graduate of TC and serving at the Harford Junior College in Bel Air, Maryland.

In 1969 Dr. Brick published *Innovation in Liberal Arts Colleges* in association with Earl J. McGrath, then a member of the TC faculty who had been a member of the Truman Commission on Higher Education (1947). Professor Brick's other writing not directly connected with community college topics was a paper for the National Foundation of Jewish Culture on *The Teaching of Judaica*. He also served as a member of the Board of Trustees of Marymount Manhattan College.

A year before his untimely death on September 21, 1974, Dr. Brick experienced a terrific spurt in his publication activities. These include *The Management of Change*, a book written with Andrew A. Busko; *Collective Negotiations in Higher Education*, Teachers College Community College Center; *Two-Year College—An Agenda for Change*, a paper for the American Association of Community Junior Colleges; and *Collective Negotiations—Strategy and Tactics*, a book he edited with seven authors including Dr. Joseph Hankin and Dr. Gordon Gee.

Over the years, Michael Brick wrote a number of founding documents for community colleges (e.g., Community College of Delaware County, Pennsylvania, and the Dundalk Community College, Maryland). He took a special delight in helping several community colleges in Florida (which were mostly attended by African Americans) improve their curricula and services.

Dr. Hankin, who preached at Michael Brick's funeral in 1974, stated in 2001, "He blended theory and practice and was a role model for the rest of us." Dr. Brick is survived by his wife, Barbara Rosen, and a son, Barrett.

CHAPTER 8

Joseph N. Hankin

An outstanding exemplar of the success of Teachers College in carrying out the goals for public community colleges set by the Truman Commission is the career of Joseph N. Hankin. For more than three decades, he has been a graduate student at TC, a fellow of the TC Community College Center, a longtime president of the Westchester Community College at Valhalla, New York, and a teacher of men and women preparing for roles as administrators or faculty in community colleges. Often in education there is a call for individuals who are both practitioners and teachers. Joe Hankin fulfills that dual role.

Born in New York City on April 6, 1940, Joseph N. Hankin was the firstborn child in his family and the first to go on to higher education. His parents were born in America of immigrants from Poland. He was educated in New York City public schools. "There were always books in the house," he noted, commenting that when he got a 98 on his report card from George Washington High School, his father wanted to know why it was not a 100.

The policy of free tuition, then a feature of City College, made it practical for him to attend this school, receiving a B.A. degree in social sciences in 1961. With a particular interest in history and a goal of seeking a career in education, Joseph Hankin obtained an M.A. in 1962 from Columbia University. His thesis was "The Progressive Party of 1924 in New York." During his master's studies at Columbia, he had taken a few courses at Teachers College and was so impressed that he enrolled in the doctoral program, specializing in community colleges. His dissertation was titled "Selected Urban

Problems and the Public Community College." He received the Doctor of Education degree in 1967.

Dr. Hankin became president of Harford Junior College in Maryland in February 1967, remaining there until shortly after its name was changed to Harford Community College four years later. On September 1, 1971, he took office as president of Westchester Community College in Valhalla, New York, a position he still holds today.

During all his years of institutional leadership, Dr. Hankin has also been preparing students for service in the community-college field. From his early years as a community-college president, he has taught courses at Teachers College. For the past twenty-five years, he has been an adjunct professor and visiting professor of adult education in the Department of Higher and Adult Education at Columbia University. For years he served as adjunct associate professor. He has taught courses, led advanced seminars, sponsored students, and served on and chaired doctoral committees. He has personified community-college administrators for generations of students and faculty at Teachers College.

In Westchester County, the New York region, and nationally, Dr. Hankin has become well known in the community-college field, not only because his TC students came from many states, but also because of his extensive writings and his involvement in many educational organizations. Given his long career as a community-college president and his vocation as an adjunct professor teaching graduate students community-college administration, it is not surprising that Dr. Hankin has written extensively and has been a frequent speaker at educational conventions. In addition, his published works include: "A Community College for Howard County" (mimeographed January 1968); "The Strategy and Tactics of Collective Bargaining" in Michael Brick's *Collective Negotiations in Higher Education*, Community College Center, Teachers College, Columbia University (1973); *Negotiating a Better Future: Planning and Organizing for Collective Negotiations in Community and Junior Colleges*, Alvin C. Eurich, Ruth G. Weintraub, and Sarah White, American Association of Community and Junior Colleges (1977); *The City Colleges of Chicago Face the 1980's: A Five Year Comparative Look at Faculty Personnel Practices in 31 Urban Community Colleges: A Report to the Board of Trustees of the City Colleges of Chicago;* "Reassessing the Commitment to Community Services," with Philip A. Fey, in *Renewing the American Community College: Priorities and Strategies for Effective Leadership*, William L. Deegan, Dale Tillery and Associates (1985); "Literature a Community College President Should Read to Be More Effective," *Community College Journal of Research and Practice* (July–August 1993); "A Thoroughly Satisfying Look at Community Colleges—Again," book review of Arthur M. Cohen and Florence B. Brawer's *The American Community College* in *Community College Week* (December 16, 1996); Remarks of MSA President Joseph Hankin on December 6, 1999, in Middle States Commission on Higher Education, *Higher Education 2000: What Will Be New? What Will Be Different?*, proceedings of The Annual Accreditation and Quality Assurance Conference, Philadelphia (2000).

Among honors received, Dr. Hankin was named one of the Hundred Most Effective College Presidents by peers in a project sponsored by the Exxon Educational Foundation in 1986. Two years later he received Teachers College's Centennial Award for dedicated service to the college.

Westchester Community College (WCC) began its institutional life a quarter century before Dr. Hankin was elected its president. It was founded as one of five technical institutes established by New York State. That state, along with California, a few other states, and a small number of cities (including Chicago), realized early on the importance of technical institutes and community junior colleges offering two years of education after high-school graduation.

The United States was facing a variety of problems in the early 1930s as the Great Depression wore on year after year. With substantial unemployment in the adult ranks, many high-school graduates had poor job prospects. Moreover, the country was moving rapidly from an economy largely based on agriculture to one increasingly dependent on science and technology. This meant that expanding numbers of high-school graduates needed technical and scientific skills to be equipped for the job market.

New York State wisely decided to locate its technical institute not far from White Plains, the county seat of Westchester County. It turned over to the trustees of the new educational institution a large and beautiful site of 218 acres in Valhalla, New York. Westchester Community College has had ample space for its building development over the past seven decades and its expansion may easily continue well into the foreseeable future.

In the early 1960s the technical institute occupied only a few, rather small buildings. These structures were adequate for the limited number of course offerings and students enrolled. In 1957 a visual arts building opened. This was followed by a spurt of construction, including the student center (1961); the technology building (1961); the physical education building (1965); the blassroom building (1966); and the library (1967).

After Dr. Hankin became president of WCC in September 1971, the first major construction was the science building (1977), followed by the academic arts building (1980). In 1976 he added adjunct teaching to his administrative duties with evening courses in community-college affairs at Teachers College, Columbia University. He still teaches these classes today.

Recent building projects at WCC are the Knollwood Center (1986), the Administration Center (1988), the Children's Center (1991), and the new bookstore and temporary library expansion (1999). In comparatively recent years, there has been a continuing expansion of computer and Internet facilities. On the main campus there are nearly seven hundred personal computers, with over twelve hundred computer stations college-wide. Other facilities are a four-hundred-seat theater, eighteen science laboratories, and sports and recreational facilities. To bring learning opportunities throughout the county, WCC has opened offsite locations in Mahopac, Shrub Oak, Port Chester, Yonkers, New Rochelle, Ossining, Mount Vernon, and the Westchester Art Workshop in White Plains and Peekskill.

The campus and physical facilities are significant for any community college but even more important are the programs, the faculty, and the students. It is to these that Dr. Hankin has devoted the bulk of his time as president of WCC, because through the interplay of these three components the success of any educational endeavor may be measured.

At the beginning of the new millennium, WCC offered over fifty different programs, grouped in five areas: engineering technologies, business programs, health sciences, public-service occupations, and liberal arts and sciences. The last category covers an essential area for the two-year college — it traditionally prepares students for transfer to the upper division of four-year colleges. Some programs in engineering technologies return to the early days of the technical institute; others have been designed to address new technology. Interest in the business programs has increased, especially in recent decades. Developments in computer technology have called for frequent updating and revision. In view of the population's growth and age, the fields served by health sciences have been expanding at a high rate. Collectively, public-service occupations provide a very large market in Westchester for well-qualified women and men.

Of the full-time faculty at WCC, 5% have bachelor degrees, about 70% have masters, and over 26% have doctorates. The male/female ratio is 60% male and 40% female, with males strongly represented in the professor rank. About 14% of the faculty are classified as minority. The faculty members are well experienced, mature, and well compensated in relation to the national averages in community colleges. These factors are understandable in view of the economic importance of Westchester County. Dr. Hankin and his associates have been careful to build and maintain a faculty at high standards. In a community college, it is essential that faculty and staff approach their work with enthusiasm and dedication and that these qualities be maintained at a high level.

In the final analysis, it is, of course, the students that are the most important element in an educational institution. It is for them that the community college exists. The challenge facing Dr. Hankin year after year is providing the best teaching to benefit the largest and most diverse group of individuals possible. Since 1946, WCC has enrolled more than three hundred thousand students. Currently about 18% of U.S. high-school graduates apply to WCC and approximately half of those who apply attend.

Total attendance during the 1999–2000 academic year was over eleven thousand credit students and a similar number in noncredit courses, with about 43% full-time and 57% part-time. Special efforts have been made to serve the diverse populations of Westchester County. Approximately five thousand students are senior citizens, about a third are minority, and some seven hundred are persons with physical disabilities. The ESL program enrolls 2,500 students. The academic spectrum runs from a large number of immigrants who are just beginning struggles with the English language to a small number who have Ph.D.'s and are seeking enrichment in some field.

A measure of WCC's success in meeting some of the local needs is that about two-thirds of the graduates remain in the county to work. As far as the curriculum is concerned, Dr. Hankin has predicted,

There will be increasing attention to life stages—those specific events which trigger a transition in one's life such as getting hired or fired, getting married or divorced, having children, getting sick, getting elected, moving to a new location, preparing for retirement or even death. . . . The predominant motivation is occupational, and since occupations will be changing rapidly throughout a student's life, it will be crucial that he or she learn how to learn. There will be more global interaction and the need to understand cultures other than our own will be obvious.

Concluding his comments on curriculum, Dr. Hankin voiced that

There will be more interaction with the corporate community and company investment in continuing education for their employees. Inservice education for professional growth of faculty will be needed to keep members from burning out and becoming overbearing to their students, especially as the average age of the faculty increases. There will be a greater number of part-time faculty members. Procedures for measuring educational accomplishment will shift away from time measurers to levels of competence and performance. Perhaps more colleges will adopt the one-course-a-month for eight or ten months so students can concentrate on a somewhat reduced academic load. Tests may change too. It has been predicted that paper tests for undergraduates will be phased out in a few years.

With a lengthy background as a community-college president—taking office at Westchester Community College when he was only thirty-one—Dr. Hankin is able to analyze the past and make some predictions for the future with considerable confidence. Moreover, being still years from becoming a "senior citizen," he will live long enough to see how accurately his projections turn out.

At a meeting sponsored by the College Board in New York City on September 11, 1998, Dr. Hankin expressed his thoughts on "The Future of Higher Education," with particular focus on community colleges. Citing a projection of the U.S. Department of Education, Dr. Hankin noted that community-college enrollment would increase 14% in the years from 1999 to 2012. This phenomenon is called a Baby Boom, similar to that between the years 1977 and 1994, which almost matched the post–World War II Baby Boom of the years 1946 to 1964. In 1946 to 1964, the number born in the United States was seventy-six million; the recent "boomlet" is about seventy-two million. The first Baby Boom resulted in the expansion of four-year colleges and the construction of almost one thousand public community colleges. The following paragraphs give Dr. Hankin's thoughts on the fundamental issues of students and the appropriate facilities to serve their needs:

Student bodies, particularly in institutions open to them, will become even more diverse than they are today, and that will have a profound impact on the delivery of services to those students. They will become older. Already in the two-year colleges the average age nationwide is 29 and soon it will be closer to the average age of the entire population which is 34.3 years. Students over 40 years of age are rapidly increasing on our campuses. Between 1970 and 1993 this enrollment grew by 235% from an estimated half million to more than 1.5 million. As the population grays and we have more educated senior citizens, more will show up on our campuses.

We will be serving a greater percent of disabled and handicapped college students. We will also serve an increasing number of students of color and international students. We will increase the number of students from lower socioeconomic groups, with all that implies about family status, income level, academic interests, and personality traits.

We can expect more immigrant students. Already my institution serves 2,500 English-as-a-second-language students per year, and in last year's graduating class, there were students born in more than 40 different countries. We can expect to serve more educated citizens. For example, in the Washington, D.C. area, at Montgomery College, Maryland, more than half of its adult students have a bachelor's degree, and at North Virginia Community College there are over 500 Ph.D.'s—not in the faculty but in the student body!

By 2018 or earlier, I predict that our community colleges will increasingly match our student population with the population of our service area and will develop appropriate programs. For me, success is when you will not be able to distinguish greatly between the general population and the student populations we serve.

Greater use of campus facilities will be made in 'off-hours' such as overnight and weekends. The Library or Learning Resource Center will take on added responsibilities and will be even more accessible than they are now. There will be a great deal more of 'distance learning.'

On changes in facilities, Dr. Hankin recalled the words of Winston Churchill, "We shape our buildings, then they shape us. . . . We must devise ways of permitting greater flexibility in the structures we already have and renovating them where necessary to permit the learning activities of the future." He also suggested that "the typical community college may be using more of its internal resources in helping to solve community problems." Staffing of outreach programs that provide education comparable to that of main campuses will be a problem.

In addition, financing will be a continuing problem for WCC and other community colleges. President Hankin noted that "tuition and fees doubled in America from 1976 to 1994 and may double again over the next 20 years." Either the colleges must develop new sources of revenue or operate more efficiently.

The Truman Commission of 1947 proposed free, public community colleges. Dr. Hankin observed in a letter to me on June 7, 2001, "As for the Truman dream of free tuition, I don't think that will happen. I was able to attend City College because the tuition was free, but society has passed this concept by. They no longer see education as an investment but rather as a cost that the individual should share in her or his future. Therefore, I believe there will be more room for private fundraising of scholarships. Here at Westchester Community College, we have just finished a $6 million campaign. The proceeds will mostly go towards scholarships. Therefore, tuition will gradually creep up and state and local shares will pretty much stay where they are—in my estimation."

As the years go on, observers of the American community-college scene will be able to make judgments concerning the accuracy of Dr. Hankin's projections. From my point of view, his predictions deserve serious consideration in the light of his long experience as a community-college president and as a teacher of students and administrators.

CHAPTER 9

Community Colleges and Research at the Turn of the Century

COMMUNITY COLLEGE RESEARCH CENTER
TEACHERS COLLEGE, COLUMBIA UNIVERSITY
MAY 2002

Community colleges are the hidden institutions of American higher education. During any given year, community colleges enroll more than one half of all credit-earning students in higher education; nevertheless, they are rarely mentioned in the newspapers, on the television, or in other forms of media. And the higher-education controversies that have preoccupied the public (such as escalating tuition costs, growing competition for admissions, affirmative action, and the neglect of teaching for research) are more relevant for four-year colleges and universities than they are for community colleges. Baccalaureate institutions also garner much of the positive publicity. Community colleges are not involved with high-profile sports, the press rarely interviews community-college experts, patients are not treated at the local community-college teaching hospital, and the public does not look to community colleges for innovative research and development to propel the country forward. For all of these reasons and despite their important roles in workforce and economic development, the value and contributions that community colleges make are often overlooked or ignored.

Academic researchers have, at best, an ambivalent attitude toward these institutions, and the large majority of academic research on community colleges over the last two decades has focused on the issue of transfer to four-year colleges. However, the most common perspective among researchers, at least until the last few years, was simply neglect.

Indeed, graduate students in several community-college leadership programs around the country do write dissertations, but most of these graduates will go on to become administrators and community-college leaders and therefore have careers that are not primarily involved with research. Other than researchers employed at community colleges themselves, only a handful of analysts and academics focus on community colleges. In the last decades, it took a diligent search through the programs of the annual conference of the American Educational Research Association (AERA) or the Association for the Study of Higher Education (ASHE) to find sessions or presentations on community colleges. Over two thousand articles appeared in the *Journal of Higher Education* (the ASHE journal) between 1950 and 2002. Of those, only seventeen had community college (or junior college) in the title. Interestingly, almost half of those (eight) appeared in the 1970s. Only four were published between 1981 and 2002.

But given the absence of attention paid to community colleges, it may appear surprising that they account for a large share of American higher education. Nearly one half of all undergraduates in postsecondary institutions in the fall of 1997 were enrolled in community colleges (U.S. Department of Education 2000b), and over the span of any given year, more for-credit undergraduate students enroll in community colleges than in baccalaureate-granting institutions. As we shall see, even these numbers fail to capture the full extent of the community college impact and role within the educational system. Nevertheless, for the most part, research on higher education has rarely been focused on this large and important sector. This neglect is perhaps even more surprising given the concentration in community colleges of poor and minority students, the types of students who normally attract the attention of education researchers.

Thus it appears that the normal concerns of education researchers about access and opportunities fade when it comes to higher education. Education researchers have focused a tremendous amount of attention on the problems of inner-city elementary schools and high schools, however if the students in those schools should be fortunate enough to go on to college, they are likely to attend a community college. Nonetheless, with regard to postsecondary education, researchers lose interest in the students whose K-12 experiences garner so much attention and concern. Postsecondary research is focused on four-year schools and, within that, on the small number of public and private elite institutions. This selective myopia is an interesting topic in and of itself.

This chapter has several goals. First I will provide some background information on the state of community colleges today, demonstrating their importance and size. Then I will outline some of the opportunities and challenges currently facing community colleges. Throughout the chapter I will argue that the research attention devoted to the colleges is not commensurate with their relative size or the important social and intellectual issues associated with their operation and development. Next I will explain why researchers have been so reluctant to study community colleges.

Much of this book describes the history of the Teachers College involvement with community colleges. During the 1960s and 1970s, the TC Center for the Study of Community Colleges engaged both in research on the colleges as well as in educating community-college administrators. This work was funded by the W. K. Kellogg Foundation and led by Walter E. Sindlinger and Michael Brick, but it waned with the end of the Kellogg funding and Sindlinger's retirement in the late 1970s. However, in the mid-1990s, community-college activities again increased at TC, carried out through the Community College Research Center (CCRC) and this time encouraged and funded by the Alfred P. Sloan Foundation. Therefore, at the end of this chapter, I will describe Teachers College's current community-college activities with an emphasis on community-college research at TC.

THE SIZE AND GROWTH OF THE COMMUNITY-COLLEGE SECTOR

In 1998 there were over 1,100 community colleges in the United States. The large majority of those institutions (almost 1,000) were public colleges. Many colleges have several campuses that operate at different levels of independence, but if branch campuses are counted, then there are now approximately 1,600 colleges, and public colleges account for an even larger share of this figure. Much of the growth of community colleges took place between 1960 and 1975, when the number of colleges (including branch campuses) grew from 390 to over 1,000 (American Association of Community Colleges [AACC] 2000, table 1.1). Student enrollment in community colleges grew even faster. In 1965 public community colleges enrolled about 1 million students, but fifteen years later, that figure had grown to just under 4 million. Over the next fifteen years, community-college enrollment continued to grow, though more slowly, reaching a peak of about 5.5 million in 1992. Enrollments then declined slightly during the 1990s, but they appear to have had a resurgence in the first two years of the twenty-first century, although national data for those years are not yet available (AACC 2000, figure 2.1).

Community-college growth relative to the growth of four-year colleges is also revealing. Enrollment in public four-year schools also grew rapidly from 3 million to 5 million (including graduate students) between 1965 and 1975, but this was a much slower growth rate than the rate for the two-year schools. The gap between the two types of schools continued to shrink, so that by 1999, 700,000 *more* undergraduates were enrolled in community colleges than in four-year public colleges. Since independent colleges are much more important in the four-year sector than among community colleges, there are still more undergraduates in four-year schools (public and private) than in two-year schools—6.8 million versus 5.4 million (AACC 2000, table 2.2).

These numbers are based on counts of the share of students enrolled in college during a given October. Community-college students are more likely than four-year students to enroll part-time or to interrupt their enrollments, therefore, if we count all students who are enrolled for credit in higher education over the course of a year (as opposed to only in October), then about 60% of all undergraduates are enrolled in two-year colleges or in two-year programs in four-year schools (Bailey, Leinbach, Scott, Alfonso, Kennedy, and Marcotte 2002). Moreover, the types of students who enroll in community colleges are precisely those students who are of most concern to scholars and policymakers. Indeed, minorities and immigrants are overrepresented in two-year schools. Community colleges are also much more likely than four-year schools to enroll first generation, postsecondary students or students from low socioeconomic backgrounds (U.S. Department of Education 2000c).

Undergraduate for-credit education is only one of the many activities that community colleges carry out. Although data on noncredit education is unreliable, community colleges have large and growing enrollments in noncredit courses. According to data collected for the National Household Education Survey, over eight million students are enrolled in noncredit courses at community colleges and public two-year technical colleges (Bailey et al. 2002). In many community colleges, more students enroll in the noncredit offerings than in the credit-bearing courses. Many individuals rely on noncredit instruction at community colleges to learn skills needed either for occupational upgrades or simply to keep up with changing work-related technology.

The colleges also carry out extensive remediation for many students who leave high school without the necessary skills for college-level work. Thus the colleges must intercede in order to address problems that high schools have been unable to solve (Perin 1998; Grubb 2001). Moreover, an increasing number of community colleges now have high schools on their campuses, conduct college-level courses at high schools (for high-school students), or enroll high-school students in their college courses diversifying even further their educational role in the community (Bailey, Hughes, and Karp 2002).

Community colleges also provide important educational opportunities for older students and those who need to work. For example, over 62% of community-college students attend part-time (AACC 2000, table 2.5), and more than 46% of community-college students are twenty-five years of age or older (AACC 2000, figure 2.2). Therefore, like four-year schools, two-year colleges provide initial full-time postsecondary education for eighteen- and nineteen-year-olds; nevertheless, they are much more likely than four-year schools to provide education for skills upgrading, career changing, or postsecondary education for adults who went to work immediately after high school.

In addition to providing educational services directly to students, the colleges have increasingly taken on a variety of activities to help local businesses. These include customized training and technical assistance as well as regional economic forecasting (Dougherty and Bakia 2000).

Community colleges are increasingly being seen as key institutions in the strength and development of their local economies.

CHALLENGES AND OPPORTUNITIES

The total enrollments and the crucial roles played by community colleges suggest that these institutions deserve much more attention from researchers than they have received thus far. Moreover, at this time, the environment in which the colleges are operating is changing rapidly. Some of these changes present significant challenges while others create some important opportunities. Given these current developments, research becomes particularly important for colleges in determining the directions that they ought to be taking, and this research may help determine the most appropriate role for community colleges within the overall system of higher education.

After several decades of growth, community colleges now face a particularly challenging environment. All of the following factors are threatening established patterns of community-college activities and potentially altering the role of the colleges within the wider landscape of higher education: changes in pedagogic and production technology; state-funding policies; the expectations of students, parents, and policymakers; demographic trends; and the growth of new types of educational institutions and providers.

As stated above, community colleges enjoyed strong enrollment growth throughout the 1960s, 1970s, and 1980s. Total fall enrollments peaked in 1992 at 5.7 million students, but they stayed around 5.4 million in 1998 (U.S. Department of Education 2000b). For the first time, colleges in many states faced declining enrollments.

Additionally, during the 1990s, state-funding priorities shifted away from higher education as prisons and health care accounted for larger shares of state budgets. Thus the share of state budgets directed to higher education shrank from 12.2% in 1990 to 10.1% in 2000 (National Association of States Budget Officers [NASBO] 2000). For example, like many state systems, the California, public, higher-education system went through a severe budget crisis early in the decade, and while the economic recovery brought some improvements to state universities and colleges, that improvement did not keep pace with overall economic growth. And as the economy faltered in the first years of the new century, higher-education budgets again came under pressure. In 2001 and 2002, many states slowed their growth and in many cases actually cut statewide higher-education expenditures.

Moreover, within the public state systems, community colleges have always had to provide an education with fewer resources per student than their four-year counterparts. For example, in the 1995–1996 school year, instructional expenditures for public community colleges stood at $3,420 per full-time equivalent student, compared with $5,486 for public colleges and $6,946 for public universities (U.S. Department of Education 2000c).

The growing movement among states to try to link funding to performance further complicates the financial outlook for community colleges. Graduation and transfer to four-year institutions are the most common indicators of performance for community colleges. By these measures, community colleges do not appear to be performing at a high level. Of all the students who entered community college in 1989, by 1994 (five academic years later) 49% had left college without a degree and only 37% had earned some kind of degree. About 15% had not received a degree, but were still enrolled (BPS89).[1] Community-college administrators, as we shall see, dispute the negative implications associated with these apparently low completion and transfer rates; nevertheless, funding based on simple graduation rates could cause serious problems for community colleges. So far, few states have implemented this policy and in those states where it has been introduced, only minimal funding is at risk. But as policymakers focus more on measurable outcomes, current graduation and transfer rates are likely to become more controversial.

Changing expectations about educational attainment will also influence community-college enrollments. Increasingly, students state that they expect to earn a bachelor's degree. In 1980, 57% of all high-school seniors believed that they either probably or definitely would graduate from a four-year college program, by 1997 that share had risen to over 77% (U.S. Department of Education 2000c). Baccalaureate aspirations have also risen among students enrolled in community colleges. In the early 1980s, about 45% of such students stated that their objective was to earn a B.A., while in the early 1990s, 70% had that goal (Schneider and Stevenson 1999). As students focus more on earning four-year degrees, we would expect to see enrollments shift toward four-year colleges. Indeed, total enrollments in these institutions did rise between 1995 and 1998 while community-college enrollments were stable, and The National Center for Education Statistics (NCES) projects that four-year enrollments will grow faster over the next decade than two-year enrollments. However, while most community-college students say that they aspire to earn a bachelor's degree, less than one quarter transfer to four-year programs (U.S. Department of Education 2000c).

To be sure, community-college transfer programs are designed to provide access to four-year programs, but policymakers and researchers continue to criticize low transfer rates. Of those first-time college students who started at a community college in 1989, about 22% transferred to a four-year school five years later (National Center for Education Statistics 2000a) and less than one tenth of students who begin in two-year colleges ever complete a bachelor's degree (Schneider and Stevenson 1999). On the other hand, many students start two-year programs without a clear intention of transferring, therefore a 100% transfer rate is not a realistic goal. Nevertheless, as the number of students who do want a four-year degree grows, there will be more pressure to increase transfer rates.

While policymakers are putting pressure on the colleges to expand their transfer rates, they are also introducing measures that will increase the number of poorly prepared students attending these colleges. Remedial or developmental courses absorb resources, and many students in regular college courses also need extra help. Although there are developmental education success stories (Hebel 1999), large numbers of poorly prepared students complicate college efforts to improve transfer and graduation rates.

Over the last two decades, the colleges' social and economic environment has changed. Other institutions, including public and not-for-profit four-year colleges, community-based organizations, for-profit companies, in-house company trainers, and even other community colleges compete with the colleges in every function that they accomplish. Many public four-year colleges have expanded their continuing education offerings, sometimes even offering full degrees, in an attempt to reach the adult and part-time students who have traditionally been served by community colleges. For-profit companies are offering short-term training, preparation for technical certifications, and full degrees at several levels. In the last few years, for-profit educational institutions such as the University of Phoenix and DeVry Institute have attracted significant attention as potential competitors. These institutions appear to have been able to attract adult students with strong occupational objectives, while in the past, community colleges prided themselves on being able to service precisely these types of students.

The potential effect of computer-based distance education is perhaps the greatest unknown concerning the nature of the competitive landscape. Certainly if distance education reduces the need for students to be at a particular place at a particular time, and does so at a reasonable cost, then the educational market will be a free-for-all. In general, research suggests that distance education is as effective at teaching substance as traditional classroom formats, although the students have to be motivated and organized. Community college professors argue that many of their students need the structure provided by the personal contact in the classroom. Whatever the problems and potentials, distance education is growing rapidly. According to data collected by the NCES, between 1995 and 1997, the share of community colleges offering distance education courses grew from 58 to 72%. The equivalent shares for public four-year institutions were 62 to 79%. Most of the rest of these colleges (two- and four-year) said that they planned to offer courses through a distance education format within three years. (By 1997, private colleges were far behind.) And during those two years, distance education enrollments more than doubled to 1.6 million, although the number of students involved was smaller since these figures represent duplicated headcounts (U.S. Department of Education 1999a).

The continued growth of computer-based distance education seems certain; nevertheless, many questions remain about the impact of those developments on different types of institutions. At this point, most of the students who participate in computer-based distance education also take regular courses at the same institution. So far, students whose only contact with an institution is through an on-line course are more rare, but what can be said is that the growth and potential of distance education has created tremendous uncertainty in higher education. Community colleges may be at a disadvantage in the on-line educational race since they have much more restricted budgets than the four-year public schools, and they lack the for-profits' access to capital markets.

POSITIVE TRENDS

While the colleges certainly face difficult challenges, several current developments are likely to increase the demand for community-college education over the next several years. First, as was emphasized above, the number of students in the typical college is projected to increase sharply over the next decade. The children of Baby Boomers (the Baby-Boom echo) are moving through their college years and are expected to expand college enrollments. The National Center for Education Statistics projects that two-year college enrollments, which stood at roughly 5,700,000 for the fall of 1999, will grow by 11 to 16% over the next decade (Gerald and Hussar 2000). This growth will benefit those colleges that still have the capacity to expand.

In addition, the growing foreign-born population in the United States will also create an increasing demand for community college education. Immigration has already had an impact on college enrollments in California. The City University of New York (CUNY), New York City's public higher-education system, was already almost 50% foreign-born in the fall of 1997, while the population of the city as a whole was about 41% foreign-born. Within the CUNY system, recent immigrants were over represented in two-year programs (Bailey and Weininger 2001).

The patterns of postsecondary enrollments have changed over the last two decades, and these trends may also benefit community colleges. Much of the policy and research about college enrollment has been dominated by a traditional conceptualization in which students attend college full-time immediately after high school and continue their enrollment uninterrupted until they graduate. This view is increasingly misleading. If we define a traditional student as one who attends college full-time and full-year until they graduate, then among students who started college for the first time in 1989, only 17% were traditional students enrolled in four-year institutions. Another 17% were traditional students who started in two-year institutions. The remaining 66% of all first-time college students could be considered nontraditional students because they attended school part-time, interrupted their studies, or changed institutions. Furthermore, this share of nontraditional students would rise further if we counted students who delayed their first-time entry into college.[2] And data from the High School and Beyond survey, which includes students who should have graduated from high school in the early 1980s, suggest that the number of nontraditional students had grown significantly during the 1980s. For example, the percentage of undergraduates who attended more than one institution increased from 40 to 54% during the 1970s and 1980s and data from the 1990s suggest that this share will have increased to over 60% during the first years of the new decade (Adelman 1999).

The growth of the importance of these diverse pathways through postsecondary education may favor community colleges that are much more oriented toward nontraditional students than four-year schools. For example, community-college students are much more likely to enroll part-time and tend to be older than four-year college students are (and therefore delayed or interrupted their enrollment). In 1998, 57% of all community-college students were enrolled part-time. And 60% of four-year college students were eighteen to twenty-four years old, while 48% of all two-year college students were in that age range (U.S. Department of Education 2000b).

Developments in technology and its effects on skill requirements will also continue to create a demand for community-college education. Projections of employment growth in different occupations and earnings trends of workers with various levels of education show that at least some education beyond high school will be necessary for workers in order to access jobs with paychecks that might support a family. While college graduates do earn more than those with an associate's degree, the value of one year of community-college education is more or less equivalent to the value of a year of education at a four-year college. The same can be said for the economic value of credits earned at the two institutions (Grubb 1999b; Kane and Rouse 1995). Between 1973 and 1998, the share of the prime-age workers with some education beyond high school but without a bachelor's degree more than doubled from 12 to 27%, while the share of the workforce that had a bachelor's degree increased from 16 to 30% (Carnevale and Desrochers 2001). While the role of associate's degrees relative to bachelor's degrees remains in flux, these trends indicate that a growing number of jobs in the economy can be effectively held by workers with postsecondary education short of a bachelor's degree.

Weak high-school preparation will also continue to create a role for community colleges that essentially gives students a second chance to prepare for college-level work. NCES judged that even among families with incomes above seventy-five thousand dollars a year, less than 60% of high-school graduates were either highly or very highly qualified for admissions to a four-year college. Another 30% of graduates were either somewhat or minimally qualified, but the levels of preparation for high-school graduates from families earning less than twenty-five thousand dollars a year was much worse. Forty-seven percent were not even minimally qualified and only 21% were either highly or very highly qualified for admissions to a four-year college (U.S. Department of Education 2000c). Forty percent of students at four-year colleges and 63% of community college students take at least one remedial course during their postsecondary enrollment (National Center for Education Statistics 2000b). Moreover, several states (including New York and Georgia) and universities (such as California State University) are now trying to limit access to four-year institutions of students who need remedial help. In the case of CUNY, remedial education is concentrated at community colleges and is being phased out of the eleven four-year colleges in the network. Thus all of these trends indicate that the community-college role in providing developmental education will continue and probably increase.

In the increasingly competitive postsecondary market, low tuition continues to be one of the community college's most important assets. This provides an important buffer against competition in states like California where full-year tuition at a community college in 1997 was less than $500. In contrast, community college tuition in New York State was over $2,500 in that year (AACC 2001).

Trends over the last twenty years suggest that the community-college tuition advantage over public four-year colleges has grown. In the

1971–1972 academic year, four-year college tuition exceeded two-year tuition by $530 (2001 dollars). That gap grew steadily over the subsequent three decades to $2,061 for the 2001–2002 year (College Board 2001).

THE COMMUNITY-COLLEGE RESPONSE

Community colleges benefit from many advantages, including low tuition, local political support, and demographic and educational trends. These benefits will continue at least for the next few years, and this will increase the potential supply of students seeking education at a community college. The growing emphasis on noncredit education and on delayed, interrupted, multiple institutional, and part-time college enrollment favors the more nontraditional history and emphasis of community colleges, at least when compared to the public and not-for-profit four-year institutions. But increasingly competitive markets, evolving student expectations, and significant changes in funding systems and pedagogic technologies have created a much more volatile and uncertain environment. How have community colleges responded to these developments?

Community-college administrators and faculty realize that their students and the public that funds them expect the colleges to provide students with opportunities to transfer to four-year colleges. Indeed, many states are implementing a variety of policies designed to facilitate transfer from both academic majors (the traditional transfer-oriented majors) and occupational majors that have conventionally been viewed as terminal community-college programs (AACC 2001). For example, several states have introduced common course content and numbering systems that guarantee that credit earned at a community college will be accepted in that state's four-year schools.

Over the past two decades, many researchers and college administrators and faculty have argued that the fundamental role of the community college is to provide more or less open access to lower division collegiate education. From this point of view, providing a transferable liberal arts education is the core function of the colleges. It is through this function that community colleges realize their mission as the nation's primary site of equal access to higher education (Eaton 1994 and 1988; Cohen and Brawer 1996; Brint and Karabel 1989).

> The collegiate community college is an extraordinary way for a demo-
> cratic society to provide the best of higher education to as many people
> as can reasonably benefit. It is a profound statement of the unique value
> this country assigns to the individual and of its faith in the future. As a
> collegiate institution, the community college is unparalleled in provid-
> ing, sustaining, and expanding educational opportunity and accomplish-
> ment within the society. (Eaton 1994, 5)

Although state agencies and college faculty and staff have worked hard to promote transfer, this has not been the primary or most promi-nent community-college response to the financial and political chal-lenges that they have faced over the past decade. Much of the energy and enthusiasm at the college level is focused on other activities. While community college presidents will articulate their commitment to trans-fer education, raising the transfer rate is rarely a college's first priority.

During the last half of the 1990s, many community-college staff turned their attention toward pedagogic issues, and this reform move-ment sought to establish and strengthen the "Learning College." Im-proving the quality of teaching may be one approach to engaging young people and addressing the criticisms that the colleges do a poor job of retaining their students. While this reformation has generated a great deal of useful discussion about teaching, so far colleges have not intro-duced, on a widespread basis, the types of institutional changes neces-sary to bring about a significant change in teaching (Grubb 1999a).

Thus many colleges, as a strategy to improve their position and bet-ter serve their constituencies, have tried to reform their current opera-tions. As another widespread response to budgetary pressure, many community colleges have sought new markets, new students, and new sources of revenues. One indication of this is the dramatic shift in the sources of community-college funds. In the past, community col-leges have depended primarily on state appropriations. In 1980, 53% of all college revenues were accounted for by this source. But by 1996, the state share of revenues had dropped to 34% (Merisotis and Wolanin

2000). The share of local revenues also fell slightly from 17.3 to 15.6%. In contrast, the revenue share accounted for by state and federal grants and contracts grew dramatically from 1% in 1980 to 18% by 1996.

In any case, almost every community college is aggressively developing its noncredit and continuing-education programs. The continuing-education catalog of a community college will show a wide array of courses, although various types of computer-related training, including preparation for IT certification exams, are increasingly common. At least in terms of the number of students (not full-time equivalent students [FTEs]), noncredit enrollments often surpass credit enrollments. Courses outside of the traditional degree programs have many advantages to the colleges, and they can be developed with fewer constraints associated with accreditation, state regulation, and faculty prerogatives. In many cases, these courses can generate budget surpluses (although in most instances, the accounting does not include the costs of classrooms and buildings and college administrative overhead). Some noncredit enrollments are generated through customized training contracts with companies. In these, specific firms contract with a college (often the resources come from state economic development funds rather than directly from the company) to provide specific training, frequently on the company site (Dougherty and Bakia 2000). While such contracts represent a minority of noncredit enrollments, they often have a high profile and carry political significance disproportionate to their size since they solidify partnerships with influential local businesses.

For the most part, continuing education and customized training operations at the colleges are organized almost independent from the credit and degree parts of the college. Sometimes space and equipment are shared, but in many cases the courses are taught off of the college campus or in separate on-site facilities. And in most cases, the continuing-education departments use different faculty. Credit and noncredit programs in similar areas may actually be in competition for students or perhaps for relationships and partnerships with local businesses that could hire graduates and provide equipment.

While community colleges have broadened their missions by seeking out new types of postsecondary students, they have also sought to expand their roles vertically—providing education to high-school students and in some cases post–associate degree students.[3] The growth of dual enrollment programs for high-school students has been one of the most talked-about trends in community colleges over the last year or two. Many colleges have enrolled hundreds of high-school students, and in some cases those enrollments have increased dramatically in just a year. College administrators, especially financial officers, are very enthusiastic about these efforts. Most of the offerings are in the social sciences and humanities and therefore do not need expensive equipment. In many cases, the courses are taught at the high schools and therefore do not require additional space. The instructors are usually adjuncts or high-school teachers, who are certified (through their educational credentials) to teach college-level courses. The colleges incur extremely low costs and are often reimbursed at the regular FTE rate. The students can usually earn *both* high school and college credit. So far, little is known about what happens to these students, but it is likely that many of them go on to four-year colleges rather than to two-year ones. These students represent a new market for the community college. Alternatively, a community college's involvement in the high school may increase the likelihood that the high-school students will choose that particular school. Therefore, the dual enrollment programs have both financial and marketing benefits to the colleges.[4]

In another trend toward vertical expansion, some colleges are also exploring the possibility of offering applied bachelor's degrees. Although this strategy has its proponents, it remains controversial and perhaps the preponderance of community college officials are skeptical. Some presidents argue that if community colleges start offering four-year degrees, their commitment to open access may be weakened. The differences in the employment conditions for faculty at two- and four-year colleges may also pose a problem to this vertical expansion of the community-college mission. Will community-college faculty working in four-year programs still be willing to teach the typically greater community-college load? Although the applied baccalaureate definitely remains controversial, the movement does seem to be gaining momentum.

As they search for new functions and markets, colleges try to find opportunities in which they can exploit the skills and the staff that they already have. For example, a strong computer science department would give a college an advantage in offering noncredit programs to prepare students for information technology certifications. Nevertheless, in many cases, there is very little coordination among programs that are substantively related. This is particularly true with regard to the coordination between credit and related noncredit programs. Often the extension or adult-education functions are housed in separate buildings, use different faculty, and are managed by their own administrators. In many cases, the developmental education function is poorly coordinated with the core substantive programs. Some educators have argued that there are important pedagogic benefits to the integration of academic and vocational education and this type of integration does appear to be a strategy to reduce the potential conflict between transfer-oriented academic programs and more applied occupational terminal degrees (Grubb 1999a). Nevertheless, while many community-college faculty members and administrators favor the integration of academic and vocational instruction, it is difficult to find well-developed programs that actually put the approach into practice (Perin 1998).

Thus community colleges have responded to the challenges that they face by building out, by seeking new markets and functions, more than by focusing on intensive efforts to improve what they are already doing. The result is that most community colleges are now institutions with multiple missions directed at addressing the needs and interests of a wide variety of constituencies. The list of missions includes transfer to a bachelor's program, terminal occupational education, developmental education, adult basic education, English as a second language, education and training for welfare recipients and others facing serious barriers to employment, customized training to specific companies, preparing students for industry certification exams, noncredit instruction in a plethora of areas (including purely avocational courses), small business development, and even economic forecasting.

RESEARCH AND THE COMMUNITY COLLEGE

As community colleges have faced these challenges, what help have they had from research? Over the past three decades, the most prominent theme in community-college research has been directly relevant to the current mission expansion strategy that the colleges have been pursuing.

Community-college critics have argued that transfer should be the central college mission and that by taking on broader functions, the colleges have weakened that core mission. In particular, they suggest that the growing emphasis on occupational education, as opposed to academic-oriented transfer programs, has a negative effect on transfer rates. According to this view, an emphasis on vocationalism draws students into programs that usually do not encourage transfer; while at the same time, vocationalism demoralizes the academic programs that encourage transfer (Dougherty 1994). Brint and Karabel (1989) argue that this function has changed the entire mission of community colleges and has turned them into vocational schools for low- and middle-class occupations, thus limiting students' opportunities for advancement. An institution established to "level up" disadvantaged segments of society has leveled down the critical literacy skills required for the degree programs. Clark (1960), in his classic work on the community college, suggested that the colleges played a functional role in adjusting (down) the expectations of students so that they would be consistent with the realities of the labor market. As the mission of the community colleges evolved to meet a broader range of needs, the earlier emphasis on liberal education and on the transfer function appeared to take a backseat to the newer demands in which vocational mission eclipsed the emphasis on transfer and liberal education (Wechsler 1968; Katsinas 1994).

While these critics oppose mission expansion because it weakens the academic transfer function, others object to the comprehensive model because it detracts from what they believe should be the core function of the community college—vocational education (Blocker, Plummer, and Richardson 1965; Grubb 1996a). A growing number of policymakers and business leaders look to occupational education at the community college as a key site for building the workforce for the next century.

Indeed, Leitzel and Clowes (1991) consider vocationalism to be the most important distinctive niche of community colleges within the system of higher education. Clowes and Levine (1989) argue that career education is the only viable core function for most community colleges. According to Grubb (1996a), the colleges and their role in society are not well served by the continued criticism of the vocational function and a strong emphasis on transfer and academics: "One implication for community colleges is that they need to take their broadly defined occupational purposes more seriously. . . . They are not academic institutions . . . even when many of their students hope to transfer to four-year colleges" (83). He argues that, 1) the emphasis on academic education implies that there is only one valued postsecondary institution, defined by the research university; 2) community colleges cannot win the academic battle because they are not selective; and 3) community colleges mostly fail in large transfer numbers, therefore their clientele is left with outcomes of uncertain academic value.

Another argument against a comprehensive strategy is more general—community colleges simply cannot do everything well and therefore must choose a limited set of objectives on which to focus. As Pat Cross asked, "can any college perform all of those functions with excellence—or even adequately in today's climate of scarce resources and heavy competition for students?" (Cross 1985, 35). After predicting growing fiscal pressures on the colleges, Breneman and Nelson (1980) made a similar argument stating that the "most fundamental choice facing community colleges is whether to emphasize the community based learning center concept, with an emphasis on adult and continuing education and community services, or to emphasize transfer programs, sacrificing elsewhere if necessary. . . . It may no longer be possible to have it both ways" (114). This perspective probably owes something to the argument that businesses must focus on their core competencies and that successful for-profit institutions of higher education tend to pursue a more focused strategy. For example, the University of Phoenix concentrates on educating adult, working students and does not try to serve the eighteen-year-old "traditional" college population. DeVry Technical Institute specializes in a small number of technical degrees and simply does not expect to enroll students interested in majoring in the humanities, the social sciences, or, indeed, many of the other sciences.

But despite these calls for more focus, community colleges and whole state systems have continued to move toward comprehensive models. Even states such as Wisconsin, which has maintained a technical college system with a primary mission of providing occupational education, have developed programs to facilitate the eventual transfer of their students to four-year programs. Few new colleges are being built, but one recent example clearly shows the appeal of the comprehensive model.

The North Harris Montgomery Community College District in Texas opened a new college — Cy-Fair College — in 2002. The college planners used several approaches to survey the needs of the community and found an interest in a wide variety of transfer and occupational courses. The college then planned to respond to almost all of those interests.

Unfortunately, research has not been able to provide a definitive measurement of the advantages and disadvantages of mission expansion. That is, arguments in favor of a more focused strategy are based on a conceptual commitment to that strategy, rather than on empirical research that shows transfer (or occupational education) is weakened by a proliferation of missions. Of course if one assumes that transfer to a four-year school is the *only* acceptable outcome for a community-college student, and that *all* current community-college students would enroll in a transfer program if those were the only programs available, then one could argue that the mere existence of nontransfer alternatives reduces transfer. But these are very bold and unrealistic assumptions that are not suggested by even the strongest transfer advocates.

Research does show that among students who state they want a B.A., those who start their postsecondary education in a community college have a lower probability of earning that degree than those who start in a four-year school. This result holds even after controlling for measured demographic characteristics (Dougherty 1994). But despite this finding, it is still unclear whether the problem is caused by the multiple-mission strategy. Research does not show that a student who would have transferred in a focused college is thwarted because the college was pursuing so many different functions. One study has suggested that while community colleges have reduced the probability of earning a bachelor's degree for some students, for other students the colleges have increased their total postsecondary education (Rouse 1995). But much more research is needed to measure these effects definitively.

Research has done a better job in explaining why community colleges reject a more focused approach in favor of a comprehensive strategy and why their response to financial pressures, both in the last few years and in earlier decades, has been to seek new markets and sources of revenue rather than to concentrate primarily on their core functions (Bailey and Morest 2002; Brint and Karabel 1989; Dougherty 1994; Grubb 1996b).

First, political factors, on the one hand, make presidents very reluctant to shed programs and, on the other, they create incentives to take on new ones. New programs have the potential to create new constituencies that in turn generate state- and local-level political support in order to maintain the flow of tax revenues. Thus even if a new program outside of a college's traditional activities loses money in an immediate sense, it may create a political environment that leads to additional reimbursements from the state, county, or local government for core activities.[5]

Second, new programs are believed to generate surpluses, and if the institution has any excess capacity (which many did have in the 1990s after a period of stable or falling enrollments), then the programs can be mounted at a low marginal cost. Even small surpluses from programs can provide presidents with discretionary funds when most of the revenues from the core credit programs are tied up in faculty salaries and other fixed costs. As state funding becomes increasingly uncertain, these alternative sources of revenue appear more attractive. This development can be seen in the dramatic growth of the share of college budgets accounted for by state and federal grants.

Moreover, it is not surprising that, in search of fresh revenues, institutions will go after new markets rather than try to increase their market share in their old activities. For example, attracting more transfer students with B.A. aspirations would require the college to convince students who previously did not enroll despite the presence of the transfer program. This might seem particularly difficult, especially as four-year colleges are trying to attract the same students; however, exploiting unserved markets seems to be easier for colleges than increasing their market share in mature markets.

Third, college administrators are not convinced that additional missions will weaken current activities. Nor do they know which ones, if they had to stand on their own, could provide a strong financial and political foundation. One of the fundamental tenets of the view that the community colleges are failed transfer institutions is that all of the new activities, particularly the growing importance of occupational education, have weakened the traditional transfer functions. Most community-college administrators reject this notion. Moreover, most colleges do not keep data or records in such a way that they could evaluate the extent of cross-subsidies or the negative (or positive) effects that one program or function has on the effectiveness of others. While it is easy to count revenues as students enroll in new programs, it is much more difficult to measure the costs, especially the strain on infrastructure and the attention of administrators, of those new programs. Thus, as was stated earlier, research has not definitively measured the costs and benefits of a comprehensive strategy. Despite the logic of the argument that one institution cannot do many things well, there is no definitive empirical evidence for this negative effect.

Thus, according to the research on the evolution of community college missions, it is not surprising that colleges have continued to move toward a more comprehensive strategy. Shedding programs risks losing visible enrollments and political support in favor of an abstract goal of focused organizational efficiency, which, though logical, lacks definitive empirical measurement and evidence.

In addition to the multiple-mission debate, researchers have also tried to directly address the controversy about low graduation and transfer rates at community colleges. The critics say that these are much too low (perhaps because of the loss of focus and too much emphasis on occupational education). Community-college administrators are much more likely to argue that students come to community colleges to learn skills and often leave when they have learned those skills even if they have not completed a degree or transferred. From this perspective, low graduation rates are as much an indication that the colleges are playing a variety of roles in their communities as they are a signal of institutional failure. Researchers have tried to determine what community-college graduation and transfer rates ought to be. What guidance have they been able to provide?

The arguments of community-college administrators suggest that there is economic value in the completion of community-college courses even if the student leaves college without a degree. Grubb (2002) reviews the research that is relevant to this and he concludes that students gain little value (in terms of increased earnings) from taking just a few courses, but that students do gain from taking a larger number of courses, even if they do not graduate. Still, students get an extra boost in their earnings from completing an associate's degree.

Another approach to determining the appropriate completion rates is to evaluate whether students achieve their stated goals. Longitudinal data collected by the National Center for Education Statistics do provide some information on student goals, and, when asked whether their primary goal in attending the current institution was to earn a degree, to transfer, or to learn skills, many community-college students state that they are there to learn skills (Bailey et al. 2002). Students in occupational programs designed to prepare students for work immediately after community college are more likely than students in transfer programs to state that they want to learn skills rather than to earn a degree or transfer. Older students are also more likely to indicate "skills" as their goal. It seems logical that older students who are more likely to have families and other responsibilities would have a more focused goal and one that could be met in a shorter amount of time. So the data on student goals appears to lend support to the argument that students are not seeking degrees.

Nevertheless, completion rates are low even among those who assert that they want a degree. Among students who enroll in a community college with the goal of earning an associate's degree, only 40% have either earned the degree or transferred to a four-year college after five years. Thirty-nine percent leave college with no degree and without transferring (Scott, Bailey, and Alfonso 2002).

Therefore, both the comparison of earnings for graduates and nongraduates, as well as the analysis of educational outcomes relative to student goals, suggests similar conclusions. Using completion rates to evaluate the performance of community colleges is somewhat misleading. Many students who do not graduate do benefit economically from their education and many do achieve their goals. Nevertheless, many fail to achieve their goals and students do benefit more from completing a degree than they would from earning the number of credits required for the degree. Colleges need to increase their graduation and transfer rates, but accountability systems need to be designed to recognize that failure to graduate cannot, in many cases, be taken as a failure by the student or the institution.

In conclusion, researchers have questioned the proliferating missions strategy increasingly pursued by community colleges, yet they have made little progress in definitively identifying the costs and benefits of that approach. They have had more success in uncovering the factors that have led to mission expansion, suggesting that the trend is not likely to be reversed without profound changes in college financing and regulation, or at least much more definitive measures of the costs and disadvantages. There is more agreement among researchers about the completion and transfer rates controversy. While there is evidence that graduation is not, and perhaps need not be, the goal of many community-college students, colleges need to increase graduation rates, both in order to improve the economic benefits that students gain from their college education as well as to help students achieve their goals. Community-college administrators and professors have not always accepted this conclusion; however, it does provide an important foundation for policy-making both at the college and at the state levels.

WHY HAVE RESEARCHERS NEGLECTED COMMUNITY COLLEGES?

This chapter has argued that community colleges comprise a large and important component of higher education. Over the course of a given year, they enroll more than one half of all for-credit postsecondary students, and these colleges are particularly important for minority and older students, for students with weak academic preparation, and for those from low-income families. Community colleges also play central roles in their local economies. Moreover, the environment in which the colleges are operating is changing rapidly; presenting both difficult challenges as well as some opportunities. These changes have implications for the general direction that the colleges take as well as their place within the overall postsecondary environment. But researchers have neglected the colleges despite the institutions' importance and the uncertainty and change facing them that make research both more useful and more interesting. Why has this happened?

Probably the most important reason is the cultural dominance of the four-year college model. "College" in the United States means attending a four-year college and "college graduation," for almost everyone, means receiving a bachelor's degree. Thus we hardly have a vocabulary with which to discuss an alternative college model. Analysts lack a cultural template within which to conceptualize the place of the community college in the system of higher education.

The overwhelming dominance of the four-year model cannot be explained by economic factors. Bachelor's degree holders do earn more money than those with an associate's degree, but that is not surprising since the B.A. takes four years while the A.A. requires only two years. But a year in a community college and a year in a four-year college result in more or less equivalent increases in earnings (Kane and Rouse 1999). Thus the value of education in these two types of institutions for a given time is roughly equivalent. Differences in the economic value of education in the two types of colleges cannot explain the conceptual hegemony of the bachelor's degree.[6]

It is telling that the success or failure of the transfer function has been, at least until recently and probably even now, the most common preoccupation of community-college researchers, particularly since the transfer function involves a conceptualization of the colleges in relation to four-year colleges. Even the scant research that has been conducted has, in effect, conceptualized the community college as the first two years of a four-year postsecondary education. Four-year colleges are not similarly judged in relation to graduate and professional schools— B.A. institutions are not criticized for failing to send most of their students on to postgraduate education.

Another reason for the lack of research on community college is certainly that most people who pursue education-research careers did not attend a community college and may have never been on a community-college campus. Their children are also unlikely to go to two-year institutions. Thus they have no direct experience with the colleges nor do they have a sense of what the colleges do or how they work. In contrast, most Americans have been through high school and, because of this, researchers have a stronger personal connection to those institutions, even to the types of inner-city schools that the researchers themselves are not likely to have attended. The effect of this lack of familiarity is accentuated because almost all active, educational researchers are employed in four-year colleges or universities. Thus they have even stronger incentives to study the problems and issues at these types of institutions. The easy availability of local data and information also plays a role.

In addition, concern about the professional status associated with studying different institutions is a factor that discourages young researchers from focusing on community colleges. Research on price fixing in the Ivy League or minority access to Harvard attracts more attention and status than state financing of community colleges or remediation at Bronx Community College. Moreover, within the field of higher education, community-college studies are seen as a specialty, much like student services or higher-education finance. Since most of the work in these latter specialties is focused on four-year schools, the field of higher education is, in effect, divided into several areas devoted to different aspects of four-year institutions and one area devoted to all community-college issues. Paradoxically, this makes community-college researchers' inquiries appear narrow since their work is confined to one area (community colleges), while researchers who focus on four-year schools appear to span several areas (student services, finance, the research/teaching conflict, etc.), even though all of them are within the four-year college sector. Researchers specializing in studies of elite research universities escape the narrow label even though community-college enrollments dwarf enrollments at the elite schools. On the other hand, elite, four-year, higher education probably does deserve more attention than its low share of student enrollment might suggest. After all, those institutions are disproportionately responsible for preparing students for graduate school, and the country's political, scientific, and cultural leaders are often educated at selective four-year schools.

Regardless, this cannot explain the research neglect of a higher-education sector that enrolls such a large share of students. Given the sociology of the research professions in this country, this trend will be reversed when colleges, universities, and research organizations (that employ researchers) and the public and private agencies and foundations (that fund research) create incentives and rewards for young researchers to devote their attention and substantial parts of their careers to studying community colleges.

To some extent this has begun to happen. Over the past five years a growing number of private foundations have increased their funding of community-college research. During 2001 and 2002, several different foundations financed meetings to discuss the development of a community-college research agenda, and grants appear to be increasing. The National Science Foundation established the Advanced Technology Education program in 1994 to conduct innovation and experimentation on technology education at community colleges, and in 2002 the College Board initiated a paid internship program to encourage graduate students to write community-college-related dissertations. Although an increase in community-college articles has not appeared in the pages of the *Journal of Higher Education*, the number of papers and sessions at the professional conferences (such as those organized by the American Education Research Association and the Association for the Study of Higher Education Research) has increased. Also, the number of papers by researchers presented at community-college conferences (such as those organized by the American Association of Community Colleges and the League for Innovation in Community Colleges) has also increased. Therefore, more researchers appear to have discovered community colleges. It remains to be seen whether this interest will be sustained or whether it will wane, as it did in the 1970s.

TEACHERS COLLEGE AND COMMUNITY-COLLEGE RESEARCH IN THE 1990s AND 2000s

In 2002 Teachers College has a substantial community-college research program organized through the Community College Research Center (CCRC) that was established in 1996. The director of the Center is Thomas Bailey, an economist on the TC faculty. The number of individuals involved in the Center fluctuates as projects begin and end, but typically, the personnel include four TC faculty, two or three full-time Ph.D. research associates, five to eight graduate students, and several support staff. In addition, CCRC works with professors and graduate students from at least five other universities and is discussing possible work with colleagues in other institutions. These include Norton Grubb, a professor at the University of California at Berkeley and one of the country's leading experts on community colleges, and Debra Bragg, a professor the University of Illinois at Urbana Champaign and the past president of the Council for the Study of Community Colleges.

The Center's associate director, James Jacobs, is also an associate vice president at Macomb Community College in Michigan.

The CCRC has conducted research on a wide variety of community-college topics. These subjects include the causes and effects of the proliferation of community college missions, remediation, accountability, distance education, workforce development, transfer, dual enrollment and other types of connections between community colleges and high schools, industry certification, the characteristics of community-college students, the educational and economic value of a community-college education, reverse transfer (students who transfer from four-year to two-year institutions), noncredit instruction, the community-college role in local economic development, the role of community colleges in the education of nurses and teachers, and counseling and student services. The CCRC has also developed an extensive Web site, where the results of this research and general information about the Center can be obtained (www.tc. Columbia.edu/ccrc).

As activity at CCRC grew, Teachers College hired Kevin Dougherty to fill a faculty position in the higher-education program. Professor Dougherty is one of the handfuls of academics throughout the country who focused their research on community colleges. The CCRC also collaborates with both the American Association of Community Colleges and the League for Innovation in Community Colleges. Since the establishment of the CCRC in 1996, researchers have conducted fieldwork at over fifty community colleges and they carry out an extensive quantitative research program based on publicly available data from the National Center for Education Statistics. The organization also has an advisory board comprised primarily of college presidents, including Joe Hankin, whose biography is presented earlier in this book. In 2002 the CCRC began planning joint research with some of its board members and other community-college staff from colleges included in the projects. In what is expected to be the first of many similar arrangements, Cythnia Heelan, the president of Colorado Mountain College and past president of the AACC, spent a sabbatical at Teachers College collaborating on a project on student services in the summer of 2002.

All of this activity has been generated by the foresight and initiative of the Alfred P. Sloan Foundation. In 1996 the Foundation invited Teachers College to write a proposal for a center to study community colleges. The Foundation staff had a simple goal. They believed that researchers were not paying enough attention to this very important set of institutions and, therefore, they decided to fund a center on community-college research at a research university.

As readers of this book now know, Teachers College has had an illustrious history of community-college-related activities, particularly in preparing community-college leaders and administrators. But that activity waned after the expiration of the Kellogg grant in the 1970s and following the 1978 retirement of Walter Sindlinger. At the time, the college was experiencing a severe drop in enrollments that resulted in shrinkage of the faculty. Although Joseph Hankin continued to teach one community-college course as an adjunct, and a few students did conduct research on community colleges, any focused effort to promote a community-college program of either training or research ceased.

Until recently, the ebb and flow of community-college activities has matched similar trends in the country as a whole. Research interest in the colleges nationally peaked in the 1970s, and other institutions dropped or sharply reduced their community-college emphases when the Kellogg Foundation ended its funding program during that decade.

Teachers College still has a long way to go before it will restore the community colleges to their previous place of prominence during the 1960s and 1970s. Although, thanks to the initiative of the Sloan Foundation, Teachers College does have a growing research portfolio, so far it has not developed an accompanying leadership education program. Perhaps thwarted by many of the same problems that have diverted research attention from community colleges nationally, within the plethora of competing educational issues, the colleges have not risen high enough among Teachers College's priorities to result in a focused institutional emphasis on the educating personnel for the sector.

Nevertheless, at this time the research focus is probably the area that needs the most attention. Besides Teachers College, there are several universities that have large and active leadership-training programs, but few others have such a large emphasis on conducting and promoting community-college research and preparing young scholars for careers devoted to the study of community colleges. Changing technology, skill requirements, demographics, and pedagogic strategies will probably continue to increase the importance and size of community colleges. These developments will benefit from a stronger understanding of how the institutions work and their effects under specific circumstances. Those interested in community colleges still have a great deal of work to do to convince researchers that the sector is worth a concentrated effort. But it appears that efforts and resources are moving in the right direction. Teachers College is well positioned to play a crucial leadership role in those developments.

NOTES

1. These numbers are based on calculations by the author using data from a Beginning Postsecondary Students (BPS:89/94) survey.

2. This data set collected by the National Center for Education Statistics includes a sample of students who entered postsecondary educational institutions for the first time in 1989. It collects data on those students through the 1993–1994 school year.

3. See Smith-Morest (forthcoming) for a full discussion of horizontal and vertical mission expansion.

4. Other institutions are beginning to take notice of this market. Administrators at one college said that their community college, the local four-year public university, and two private, not-for-profit colleges were all offering courses in one local high school.

5. For example, one of the reasons that a community college I visited in 2001 had introduced a dual enrollment program with local high schools was to build political support among local taxpayers for additional local revenues.

6. In investment terms, a $1,000 investment at a 10% interest rate will earn $100, while a $2,000 investment at the same interest rate will earn $200. In terms of the returns for a dollar invested, these two investments are equivalent even though the investor who put up $2,000 will earn more money.

REFERENCES

Adelman, C. 1999. *Answers in the tool box: Academic intensity, attendance patterns, and bachelor's degree attainment.* Washington, D.C.: U.S. Department of Education.

American Association of Community Colleges (AACC). 2000. *National profile of community colleges: Trends and statistics*, 3rd edition. Washington, D.C.: Community College Press.

———. 2001. *State-by-state profile of community colleges, 2000*. Washington, D.C.: Community College Press.

Bailey, T. R., and I. E. Averianova. 1998. *Multiple missions of community colleges: Conflicting or complementary.* New York: Community College Research Center, Teachers College, Columbia University.

Bailey, T. R., K. Hughes, and M. M. Karp. 2002. *What role can dual enrollment play in easing the transition between high school and postsecondary education?* Washington, D.C.: Office of Vocational Education, U.S. Department of Education.

Bailey, T. R., T. Leinbach, M. Scott, M. Alfonso, B. Kennedy, and D. Marcotte. 2002. *The characteristics of occupational sub-baccalaureate students.* Washington, D.C.: U.S. Department of Education.

Bailey, T. R., and V. S. Morest. 2002. *Causes and consequences of multiple missions of community colleges.* New York: Community College Research Center, Teachers College, Columbia University.

Bailey, T. R., and E. Weininger. 2001. *Performance, graduation, and transfer of immigrants and natives in CUNY community colleges.* New York: Community College Research Center, Teachers College, Columbia University.

Blocker, C. E., W. Plummer, and R. C. Richardson Jr. 1965. *The two-year college: A social synthesis.* Englewood Cliffs, N.J.: Prentice-Hall.

Breneman, D. W., and S. C. Nelson. 1980. The community college mission and patterns of funding. In *New directions for community colleges*, ed. D. W. Breneman and S. C. Nelson, 73–81. San Francisco, Calif.: Jossey-Bass.

Brint, S., and J. Karabel. 1989. *The diverted dream: Community colleges and the promise of educational opportunity in America, 1900–1985.* New York: Oxford University Press.

Carnevale, A. P., and D. M. Desrochers. 2001. *Help wanted . . . Credentials required.* Princeton, N.J.: Educational Testing Service.

Clark, B. 1960. The 'Cooling Out' function in higher education. *American Journal of Sociology* 65:569–576.

Clowes, D. A., and B. H. Levine. 1989. Community, technical, and junior colleges: Are they leaving higher education? *Journal of Higher Education* 60:349–356.

Cohen, A., and F. B. Brawer. 1996. *The American community college.* San Francisco: Jossey-Bass Publishers.

College Board. 2001. Trends in college pricing 2001. Washington, D.C.: Author.

Cross, K. P. 1985. Determining missions and priorities for the fifth generation. In *Renewing the American community college: Priorities and strategies for effective leadership*, ed. W. Degan and D. Tillery, 34–52. San Francisco: Jossey-Bass.

Dougherty, K. J. 1994. *The contradictory college: The conflicting origins, impacts, and futures of the community college.* Albany: State University of New York Press.

Dougherty, K., and M. Bakia. 2000. Community colleges and contact training: Content, orgins and impact. *Teachers College Record* 102:197–243.

Eaton, J. S., ed. 1988. *Colleges of choice: The enabling impact of the community college.* New York: American Council on Education: Macmillan Publishing Company.

——, ed. 1994. *Colleges of choice: The enabling impact of the community college.* New York: American Council on Education: Macmillan Publishing Company.

Gerald, D. E., and W. J. Hussar. 2000. *Projections of education statistics to 2010.* Washington, D.C.: U.S. Government Printing Office.

Grubb, W. N. 1996a. *Working in the middle.* San Francisco: Jossey-Bass.

——. 1996b. *Workforce, economic, and community development: The changing landscape of the entrepreneurial community college.* Mission Viejo, Calif.: League for Innovation in the Community College.

——. 1999a. *Honored but invisible: An inside look at teaching in community colleges.* New York: Routledge.

——. 1999b. *Learning and earning in the middle: The economic benefits of sub-baccalaureate education.* New York: Community College Research Center, Teachers College, Columbia University.

——. 2001. *From black box to Pandora's box: Evaluating remedial/ developmental education.* New York: Community College Research Center, Teachers College, Columbia University.

——. 2002. Learning and earning in the middle, part I: national studies of pre-baccalaureate education. *Economics of Education Review* 21:299–321.

Hebel, Sara. 1999. Community college of Denver wins fans with ability to tackle tough issues. *Chronicle of Higher Education* (7 May):A37.

Kane, T. J., and C. E. Rouse. 1995. Labor-market returns to two- and four-year college. *American Economic Review* 85:600–614.

——. 1999. The community college: Educating students at the margin between college and work. *Journal of Economic Perspectives* 13:63–84.

Katsinas, S. G. 1994. Is the open door closing? The democritizing role of the community college in the post-Cold War era. *Community College Journal* 64, no. 5:24–28.

Leitzel, T. C., and Clowes, D. A. 1991. The diverted dream revisited. *Community Services Catalyst* 24, no. 1:21–25.

Merisotis, J. P., and T. R. Wolanin. 2000. *Community college financing: Strategies and challenges.* Washington, D.C.: Community College Press.

National Association of State Budget Officers. 2000. *State expenditure report.* Washington, D.C.: NASBO.

National Center for Education Statistics. 2000a. *Beginning Postsecondary Students Longitudinal Study, 1989–94* (BPS:1989–1994) datafile.

———. 2000b. *High School & Beyond Longitudinal Study of 1980 Postsecondary Education Transcript Study* (HS&B:So PETS) datafile.

Perin, D. 1998. *Curriculum and pedagogy to integrate occupational and academic instruction in the community college: Implications for faculty development.* Community College Research Center, Teachers College, Columbia University.

Rouse, C. E. 1995. Democratization or diversion? The effect of community colleges on educational attainment. *Journal of Business and Economic Statistics* 13:217–224.

Schneider, B., and D. Stevenson. 1999. *The ambitious generation: America's teenagers motivated but directionless.* New Haven: Yale University Press.

Scott, M., T. Bailey, and M. Alfonso. 2002. *Educational Outcomes of Occupational Post-Secondary Students.* Washington, D.C.: U.S. Department of Education.

Smith-Morest, V. Forthcoming. Integrating Multiple Missions of Today's Community Colleges. *Community College Review.*

U.S. Department of Education, National Center for Education Statistics. 1999a. *Distance education at postsecondary education institutions, 1997–98.* NCES 2000-013. Washington, D.C.: U.S. Government Printing Office.

———. 1999b. *Participation in adult education in the United States, 1998–99.* Washington, D.C.: U.S. Government Printing Office.

———. 2000a. *Integrated Postsecondary Education Data System (IPEDS), "Completions" survey,* datafile.

———. 2000b. *Integrated Postsecondary Education Data System (IPEDS), "Fall Enrollment" survey,* datafile.

———. 2000c. *The condition of education 2000.*

Wechsler, H. 1968. *The transfer challenge: Removing barriers, maintaining commitment.* Washington, D.C.: Association of Community Colleges.

Grayson N. Kefauver

George Drayton Strayer

Mildred Montag, nursing educator

Ralph R. Fields, two-year college generalist

Earl McGrath, national pacemaker

Hollis Caswell, presidential leader

Walter E. Sindlinger, Mr. Community College I

Michael Brick, Mr. Community College II

Harland G. Bloland, community college dissertation advisor

Richard Anderson, community college dissertation advisor

Joseph N. Hankin, longtime community college president and TC professor

James L. Bess, TC professor in higher education in the 1970s

Kevin J. Dougherty, TC professor teaching in community college field

Thomas R. Bailey, director, TC Community College Research Center

Thomas Bailey, Martin Quigley, and Arthur Levine in President Levine's office at Teachers College, Columbia University

Appendix A

BIOGRAPHIES OF TEACHERS COLLEGE FACULTY AND ALUMNI INVOLVED IN COMMUNITY COLLEGES

Deloris N. Aleksandras
201 East Wilmette Avenue, Palatine, SC 60067–7248, (847) 358–4583.
b. Odell, IL, Sept. 1, 1912. e. Augustana Sch. of Nursing, 1948–51;
Loyola, p/t; TC, 1957–60; N. Illinois, p/t.
Employment: TC, 1959–60; N. Chicago V.A. Hosp., 1960–65;
Amundsen Mayfair CC, 1965–67; Elgin CC, 1967–78; College Of
Lake County, 1979–87.

Virginia O. Allen
82B Dorset Lane, Monroe Township, NJ 08831, (609) 655–4641,
red.voa@juno.com. b. Somerville, NJ, Aug. 15, 1929. e. Monmouth
Med. Ctr. Sch. of Nursing, 1948–51; Seton Hall, B.S., 1952–55; TC,
M.A., 1957–59, E.D.D., 1975–77.
Employment: head nurse, Monmouth Med. Ctr., NJ, 1951–52; instr.,
Cooperative Research Project, NJ, 1953–57; camp nurse, Camp Echo
Hill, NJ, 1954–55; health coord., Mid Pacific Inst., HI, 1957–58; chair
and assoc. prof., Newton Jr. Coll., MA, 1964–68; assoc. dir. and con-
sultant, Natl. League for Nursing, NY, 1963–64; chair and prof., U. of
Vermont, 1968–78; dean, Marshall U., WV, 1978–80; dir., council of
assoc. degree programs, Ntnl. League for Nursing, 1980–82; dir., div.
of accreditation svcs., Natl. League for Nursing, 1981–84; exec. sec.,
NYS Board for Nursing and Admin. of Nursing Educ. Unit, NYS

Educ. Dept., 1984–86; chair, Dept. of Nursing, Middlesex County Coll., NJ, 1986–89; received the Award for Distinguished Achievement in Nursing Education from N.E.A.A., TC, 1973.

Publications: "Improving Communication," *Nursing Outlook*, 1962; *Community College Nursing Education*, 1971; "Associate Degree Graduates—Generalists or Specialists?" *Journal of Nursing Education*, 1974.

Guy Altieri
1052 Cutler Circle, Saline, MI 48176, (734) 429–0725, galtieri@wccnet.org; exec. VP for instruction, Washtenaw CC, 4800 East Huron River Drive, PO Box D1, Ann Arbor, MI 48106–1610. b. Philadelphia, PA, July 25, 1950. e. Rowan Coll., B.A. (sociology), 1972; Bath U., 1971; Rowan Coll., M.A. (CC teaching-sociology), 1973; West Chester U., M.A. (psychology), 1980; Columbia U., M.A. (adult educ. admin.), 1985, Ed.D. (higher educ.), 1987.

Employment: instr., Rowan College, 1973; instr., Atlantic CC, 1973; instr., Camden County Coll., 1972–74; instr., Wilmington Coll., 1974–75; instr., Salem CC, 1974–79; coord. of developmental studies, Salem CC, 1976–78; chair, dept. of educ. development, Salem CC, 1977–79; dir. of instruction, Salem CC, 1980–84; dean of academic affairs, Salem CC, 1980–84; acting pres., Salem CC, 1982; VP and dean of academic affairs and student svcs., Salem CC, 1984–87; VP of instruction and student svcs., Washtenaw CC, 1987–99; instr., Eastern Michigan U., 1989–present; instr., Washtenaw CC, 1995–present; exec. VP for instruction, Washtenaw CC, 1999–present.

Traci D. Anderson
4707 East McDowell Road, Phoenix, AZ 85008, (602) 745–8042, worthyprof@netscape.net. b. Nanuet, NY. e. Howard U., B.A., 1993; TC, M.A., 1995.

Employment: instr., Katharine Gibbs Bus. Sch., 1995–97; adjunct prof., Coll. of New Rochelle, 1997; adjunct prof., CUNY, 1996–97; educ. coord, Police Athletic League, 1998; proj. mgr./curriculum coord., U. Of Phoenix, 1998–99; prof. of English, Maricopa CC, 1998–present.

Publications: "My Brother," "Bourgeois in the Boroughs," in *Obsidian: Black Literature in Review*, 1995.

Jean M. Arnold

4735 Starboard Drive, Bradenton, FL 34208, (941) 746–6434, jeanmargaret@worldnet.att.net. b. Springfield, MA, Jan. 3, 1941. e. Burbank Hosp. Sch. of Nursing, 1962; Fitchburg State Teachers Coll., B.S.E., 1962; Boston U., M.S., 1965; TC, Ed.D., 1975.

Employment: faculty committee, Thomas Edison State Coll., 1986–present; assoc. prof., Rutgers U., 1979–98; faculty consultant, Excelsior Coll., 1997–present; prof. emerita nursing, Rutgers U., 1998–present.

Publications: Computer Applications in Nursing Education and Practice, co-editor with G. A. Pearson, ed., 1992 (received American Journal of Nursing Book of the Year Award); "Nursing Informatics Educational Needs," *Computers in Nursing* 14 (1996); "Comparison Use of Nursing Language in Documentation of Rehabilitation Nursing," in *Classification of Nursing Diagnoses*, M. J. Rantz and P. LeMone, eds., 1999.

Natalie Marks Asouline

2402 Antiqua Creek, #DI, Coconut Creek, FL 33066, (954) 977–0058, nasouline@hotmail.com. b. New York, NY., May 11, 1924, e. U. of Cincinnati, B.S., 1944–47; Columbia U., M.A., 1953–55; Alfred Adler Inst. for Individual Psychology, 1956–58.

Employment: psychiatric nurse, Nassau CC, 1969–87.

Sylvia Barker

788 Columbus Avenue, #6K, New York, NY 10025–5942, (212) 864–3398. b. Glens Falls, NY, Sept. 11, 1914. e. Green Mountain Jr. Coll., 1933; Mount Sinai Hosp. Sch. of Nursing, 1936; TC, B.S., 1947, M.A. 1951.

Employment: Mount Sinai Hosp., NY, staff nurse, medical surgical nursing, 1936–37; head nurse, gynecology, 1937–40; asst. instr., nursing arts, 1940–41; instr., children's nursing, 1941–45; instr. in charge, nursing arts, 1945–48; supervisor, children's nursing, 1951–66; asst.

dir., inservice education, 1966–72; assoc. dir. of nursing, 1972–77; assoc. dir, nursing affairs, 1977–86; consultant, nursing admin., 1986–94; Michael Reese Hosp., IL, instr. in charge, nursing arts, 1948–50.

Publications: "Pediatrics, Family Style," *AJN*, 1958; "Risk Management," *New York State Nurses Association Journal*, 1983; "Seminar on the Prevention and Management of Falls," *The Mount Sinai Nurse*, 1992.

Roslyn Benamy
295 Churchill Road, Teaneck, NJ 07666, (201) 837–3054, rosbenamy@aol.com. b. New York, NY, May 24, 1929. e. NYU, B.S., 1954; NYU, M.B.A., 1957; TC, M.A.T., 1985.
Employment: professor emeritus, Rockland CC.

Marianne Berel
76 Riverside Drive, New York, NY 10024, (212) 874–7786. b. Breslau, May 28, 1911. e. TC, B.A., 1961; TC, M.A., 1966; TC, Ed.M., 1973.
Employment: learning disability therapist, United Cerebral Palsy Inc. of NYC, 1966–93.

Publications: Bibliography on music therapy for handicapped children, 1971; "Music as a Facilitator for Visual Motor Sequencing Tasks in Children with Cerebral Palsy," in *Developmental Medicine & Child Neurology*, Dr. Diller and M. Orgel, 1971; "The Use of Music to Facilitate Learning in a Class with Multihandicapped Children," videotape, 1976; "Teaching Mathematics to a Multihandicapped Boy, a Case Study," *The British Society for the Study of Mental Subnormality*, 1976; "Teaching Mathematics to a Multihandicapped Girl, a Case Study," *International Journal of Rehab*, 1978; *The Application of a Color Sequence to Teach Mathematics to a Multihandicapped Girl*, videotape/case study, Don Brockway, 1979; "Child's Play," *USA Toy Library Association*, 2000.

Margaret C. Berry
4100 Jackson Avenue, #425, Austin, TX 78731, (512) 345–3726, mcberry@mail.utexas.edu. b. Dawson, TX, Aug. 8, 1915. e. U. of Texas at Austin, B.A., 1933–37; Columbia, M.A., 1939–43, Ed.D., 1965.

Employment: high-school history instr., 1937–47; asst. dean/registrar and history instr., Navarro Jr. Coll., TX, 1947–50; dean of women, East Texas State U., 1950–60; instr., U. of Texas at Austin, 1962–80.

Publications: wrote four books about the history and student culture of U. of Texas.

Barbara (Bobbi) J. Brauer

51 Reed Drive, Roslyn, NY 11576, (516) 248–2019, bjb45@aol.com; dir. College Now Program, Queensborough CC, 222–05 56th Avenue, Rm. L440, Bayside, NY 11364–1497. b. New York, NY, Oct. 5, 1951. e. Brandeis, B.A., 1968–72; TC, M.A., 1972–73.

Employment: Admitting Office intern, Madison Avenue Hosp., NY, 1968–71; instr., Temple Sholom, MA, 1971–71; instr., Oak Hill elem. sch., MA, 1972; admissions asst., CUNY, 1973; asst. to assoc. dean of faculty, BMCC–CUNY, 1973; coord. of transfer counseling, BMCC, CUNY, 1973–76; coord. alumni relations, BMCC–CUNY, 1977; academic advisor and asst. prof., BMCC–CUNY, 1977–79; coord. of transfer counseling and adjunct asst. prof., BMCC–CUNY, 1979–80; PTA exec. board member, Herricks school district, NY, 1983–91; general counselor and adjunct asst. prof., Queensborough CC–CUNY, 1993–95; honors scholarship coord. and adjunct asst. prof., BMCC–CUNY, 1992–97; dir., College Now Program, Queensborough CC–CUNY, 1998–present.

Publications: Academic Advisement Bulletin (BMCC), 1975–76; *Scholarship Update* (BMCC), 1992–97; *College Now* (Queensborough CC), 1999.

Patricia R. Brewer

6976 Old Troy Pike, Huber Heights, OH 45424, (937) 233–6970, patricia.brewer@sinclair.edu; asst. to VP for instruction, Sinclair CC, 444 West 3rd Street, Dayton, OH 45402. b. Wilmington, OH, Mar. 1, 1953. e. Wilmington, OH, B.A., 1974; Ball State, M.A., 1982; TC, Ed.D., 1998.

Employment: academic coord. and grantsperson, Wilmington Coll., OH, 1980–82; registrar and dir. academic programs, Chatfield Coll., OH, 1982–85; general studies counselor, Indiana U. East, 1986–87;

education/career counselor, Educational Opportunity Ctr., OH, 1987; asst. to VP for instruction, Sinclair CC, OH, 1988–present; president, Adult Higher Education Alliance, 1999–2000.

Publications: "Learner Outcomes as Articulated in Adult Education Literature: An Annotated Bibliography," *ERIC*, 1996; "General Education: Starting and Restarting," with L. Denney and W. Struhar, *ERIC*, 1998; "Learning Styles Assessment," in *Developing Adult Learners: Strategies for Teacher and Trainer*, M. Fiddler, C. Marienau, and K. Taylor, 2000.

Eileen Pennino Brown, Ed.D.

Employment: professor, Norwalk CC, 1983–99; chairperson, NCC Social Science Dept., 1990–94.

Publications: "Norwalk CC AA-AS Degree Review Committee Curriculum Report," *ERIC*, 1989; *Integrated Skills Reinforcement in the College Classroom, Assessment Update*, 1992; book reviews in *TC Record* of *The Meaning of General Education*, G. Miller, 1991, and *Rethinking the College Curriculum: Toward and Integrated Interdisciplinary College Education*, M. Clark and S. Wawrytko.

Elsie Gee Campbell

b. Bakersfield, CA, Dec. 24, 1928. d. Bakersfield, CA, Mar. 1, 2001. e. Bakersfield Coll., 1946–47; UC Berkeley, 1947–48; UC San Francisco, B.S., 1951; TC, M.A., 1959.

Employment: nurse, Mercy Hosp., CA, 1951–52; nurse, Queen's Hosp., HI, 1952–53; nurse, UC Hosp., San Francisco, 1953–55; instr., Middletown State Hosp., NY, 1955–59; prof. nursing, Bakersfield Coll., 1959–60 and 1965–89; instr., Auburn Hosp. Sch. of Nursing, NY, 1960–61; instr., Ithaca Sch. of Practical Nursing, NY, 1961–64.

Brian G. Chapman

1548 Hawthorne Avenue, Columbus, OH 43203, (614) 253–8169, bgctexas@aol.com; enrollment services administrator, Columbus State CC, 550 East Spring Street, Madison 225, Columbus, OH 43215. b. Springfield, MA, Dec. 28, 1964. e. Greater Hartford CC, 1989–90; Central Connecticut State, B.S., 1994; TC, M.A., 1996; U. of Texas at Austin, Ph.D., 2001.

Employment: special asst. to VP of acad. affairs, U. Conn. at Santa Monica Coll.; instr. in a TRIO program; Kellogg fellow in the CC Leadership Program reporting on model community colleges nationwide, U. of Texas at Austin, 1997.

Publications: "Addressing the Needs of Students on Scholastic Probation," *Innovation Abstracts*, 19; "Concurrent Enrollment as a Strategy to Meet Urban Educational Needs," *Innovation Abstracts*, 22; "Systems for Offering Concurrent Enrollment in High School and Community Colleges," *New Directions for Community Colleges.*

Mary Lea (Azcárraga) Christensen
6903 SE Riverside Drive, #19, Vancouver, WA 98664, (360) 693–3456. b. Panamá, R.P., Sept. 26, 1931. e. Canal Zone Junior Coll., 1951; TC, M.A., 1963; Columbia-Presbyterian Sch. of Nursing, 1958.

Employment: instr., Community Health Nursing, U. of Oregon Health Sciences Center, 1974–76.

Xenia A. Christiansen
569 Crowell Road, North Chatham, MA 02650, (508) 945–2915, xeniachris@msn.com. b. Aruba, Feb. 28, 1932. e. Bronx HS of Science, 1947–50; Adelphi, NY, B.S., 1950–54; TC, M.A., 1957–59.

Employment: instr., St. Luke's Hosp. Sch. of Nursing, 1962–63; instr., Cape Cod Hosp. Sch. of Practical Nursing, 1965–71; prof. of nursing, Cape Cod CC, 1971–97; prof. emeritus, Cape Cod CC, 1997–present.

Clifton Clarke
4624 Avenue K, Brooklyn, NY 11234, (718) 434–8916, cliff@lagcc.cuny.edu; assoc. dean of institutional planning and special asst. to the president, LaGuardia CC–CUNY, 31030 Thomson Avenue, Long Island City, NY 11101. b. Jamaica, W.I., Oct. 6, 1948. e. Coll. of Arts, Science and Technology, Jamaica, W.I.; Mico Teachers Coll., Jamaica, W.I.; Brooklyn Coll.–CUNY, B.S., M.A.; TC, M.Ed., Ed.D.; SUNY, C.P.A.

Employment: dir. sports and science teacher, Camperdown HS, Jamaica, W.I., 1970–72; dir. education and research, Bustamente Industrial Trade Union, Jamaica, W.I., 1972–80; asst. accountant, Holmes Medical Supply, 1980–83; auditor/tax accountant, Mitchell, Titus

& Co., NY, 1983–85; sr. commercial financial examiner, Bank Leumi Trust Co., NY, 1985–86; sr. commercial financial examiner, Bankers Trust Co., NY, 1986; LaGuardia CC, asst. prof., 1986–89, assoc. prof., 1989–92, asst. to the dean for academic affairs, 1989–94, prof., 1992–present, exec. assoc. to VP/provost, 1994–98; assoc. dean for institutional planning and special asst. to the president, 1999–present.

Publications: "Integrating Ethics in Accounting Programs," *Community Review*, 1990; "Affirmative Action in Higher Education: A Case for Clarity," *Community Review*, 1996; "Dynamic Planning: Building Organizational Capabilities in Mature Institutions of Higher Education," *Community Review*, 2001.

Nancy Elaine Clarkson
6897 Gillis Road, Victor, NY 14564, (716) 924–9886, bargainhunter3@ aol.com; assoc. prof. of nursing, Fingerlakes CC, 4355 Lakeshore Drive, Canandaigua, NY 14424. b. Rochester, NY, Mar. 13, 1949. e. Keuka Coll., B.S., 1971; TC, M.E., 1979.

Employment: Highland Hosp. Sch. of Nursing, NY, 1974–77; Keuka Coll., NY, 1981–82; Fingerlakes CC, 1983–present.

Publications: "Drugs and Nursing Implications," *NSNA NCLEX-RN Review*, A. Stein and J. Miller, eds., 2000; regularly compiles two monthly continuing-education tests in *RN Magazine*.

Pat Feltz Cohen
21731 Saluda Circle, Huntington Beach, CA 92646–8224, patcohen@ surfside.net; program mgr., UC Irvine, 224 Irvine Hall, Irvine, CA 92697–7555, (949) 824–5644. b. Indiana, June 7, 1932. e. Indiana U., B.S.; TC, M.A., Ed.M.

Employment: instr., UCLA; consultant, Nurseco, Inc., CA; coord. of educ., Doctors & Nurses Home Nursing Care, CA; program mgr., American Cancer Society, CA, 1990–93; med. educ. coord., Bristol Park Medical, CA, 1993–94.

Publications: six *Nursing Care Planning Guides*, 1974–86.

John J. Connolly
PO Box 97, Waccabuc, NY 10597, (914) 763–6638, jconnolly@castleconnolly.com; president and CEO, Castle Connolly Medical, Ltd., 60 East 56th Street, New York, NY 10022, (212)

980–8230, x23. b. Worcester, MA, Feb. 4, 1940. e. Worcester State, B.S., 1962; U. Conn, M.A., 1963; TC, Ed.D., 1972.

Employment: science teacher, Worcester Board of Educ., MA, 1963–64; guidance counselor, Worcester Board of Educ., MA, 1963–64; dir. of admissions and registrar, Sullivan County CC, 1964–67; asst. dean and dir. community services, Mercer County CC, 1967–69; dean, Harford CC, 1969–72; president, Dutchess CC, 1972–81; president, NY Medical Coll., 1981–91; chairman of the American Assoc. of Community and Junior Colleges, 1975.

Mary P. "Mollie" Cook

1212 Ash Street, Denver, CO 80220, (303) 355–9574. b. Pittsburgh, PA, Feb. 20, 1931. e. U. of Pittsburgh, B.S.N., 1954; TC, M.A., 1958; attended classes at CC of Aurora, CO, 1988–89.

Patricia Dewerth Corbett

54 Indian Hill Road, Winnetka, IL 60093, (847) 256–5088, pcorbett@ xsite.net; prof. and chair of nursing, Harry S. Truman Coll., 1145 West Wilson Avenue, Chicago, IL 60640. b. Milwaukee, WI, June 30, 1941. e. Coll. of St. Teresa, MN, B.S., 1959–63; TC, M.Ed., 1966–68.

Employment: Cornell U./New York Hosp. Sch. of Nursing, 1968–70; asst. prof. of nursing, Bronx CC, 1970–72; asst. prof. and chair of nursing, Harry S. Truman/Mayfair Coll., IL, 1972–present.

Florence Coslow

358 Russett Road, Chestnut Hill, MA 02467, (617) 469–0524. b. Sharon, PA, Aug. 25, 1931. e. Beth Israel Hosp. Sch. of Nursing, MA, 1949–52; Simmons Coll., MA, B.A., 1953–54, nurse practioner, 1974; TC, M.A., 1961–62.

Employment: instr., Beth Israel Hosp. Sch. of Nursing, 1957–61; asst. prof., Newton Jr. Coll., MA, 1962–72; sr. nurse clinician, Harvard Community Health Plan, 1976–96.

Publications: "The ADN Faculty," *Technical Nursing—Dimensions and Dynamics*, 1972; "Clinical Application of Relaxation Techniques in Ambulatory Care Practice," *Nurse Practitioner Journal*, 1983; "The Nurse Practitioner in the HMO," *HMO Practice*, 1992; "The New Breed of Nurse Practitioners," *Journal of Health Care Benefits*, 1993; "Nurse Practitioners Sponsor Women's Health Conference," *HMO Practice*, 1994.

Lois L. (Goldman) Cowan
4 Leone Close, Scarsdale, NY 10583, (914) 725–5235. b. Miami, FL, Jan. 7, 1924. e. Wesleyan Coll., GA, B.A., 1941–45; TC, M.A., 1946, Ph.D., 1951; U. of Florida, 1946; Harvard U., 1948.

Employment: instr., Florida State U., 1946–49, involved in a statewide community-college movement, traveling to various locations to teach on a revolving basis; asst. dean of students, Hunter Coll., CUNY, 1950–52; instr./volunteer (domestic violence prevention at the high-school level), NY State Dept. of Educ., 1980–95; Westchester CC Foundation, 1998.

Stephen A. Curto
4 Madaline Drive, Edison, NJ 08820–1127, (908) 757–8072; scurto@brookdale.cc.nj.us; chair, counseling division and associate prof., Brookdale CC, Lincroft, NJ 07738. b. Newark, NJ, Feb. 25, 1948. e. Marist Coll., NY, B.A., 1969; TC, M.A., 1972, Ed.D., 1981.

Employment: counselor, Queensborough CC, 1972–74; project coord., CUNY Research Foundation, 1972–74; Adelphi U., 1972–77; TC, 1977–80; NY Institute of Technology, 1980–81; Brookdale CC, NJ, 1981–present; licensed NJ psychologist with private practice and consulting work with Manchester, Inc.—Partners International; currently developing the NJ Coastal Communiversity (Brookdale CC) and the Multi-Institutional Teaching Center.

Marcia A. Dake
7442 Spring Valley Drive, Springfield, VA 22150, (703) 451–6407, MAD7442@aol.com. b. Bemus Point, NY, May 22, 1923. e. Crouse Irving Hosp., 1944; Syracuse, B.S., 1951; TC, M.A., 1956, Ed.D., 1958.

Employment: dean and prof., U. of Kentucky Coll. of Nursing, 1958–71 (developed assoc. deg. nursing programs in seven community college systems); dean and prof., James Madison U. Coll. of Nursing, 1979–88.

Rose M. Channing Danzis
5055 Collins Avenue, #8C, Miami Beach, FL 33140, (305) 866–7953, (732) 744–9750. b. Adrian, PA, Sept. 12, 1920. e. Jersey City Hosp. Sch. of Nursing, 1949; NYU, B.S.N., 1954; TC, M.A., 1961, M.Ed., 1971, Ed.D., 1973.

Employment: apprentice librarian, Perth Amboy Public Library, 1937–39; secretary, American Smelting & Refining Co., 1940–42; Public Health Nursing Service of Jersey City, staff nurse, 1949–51, asst. district supervisor, 1951–55; Charles E. Gregory Sch. of Nursing, dir. health and recreation, 1958–59, clinical coord., 1959–61, assoc. dir. of nursing educ., 1961–66; Middlesex County Coll., chair, dept. of nurse educ., 1966–69, dir. div. of health technologies, 1969–72, dean, div. of health technologies, 1972–78, president, 1978–86; president, Assoc. of County Community College Presidents, NJ, 1983–85; member, board of directors, American Assoc. of Comm. and Jr. Colleges, 1984–86.

Publications: "Nursing Education at Middlesex County College," *New Brunswick Daily Home News*, 1966; "Nursing Education and Nursing Practice in Modern Partnerships for Today and the Future," *New Jersey State Nurses Association Perspectives*, 1977; "International Business Education in New Jersey Community Colleges," paper presented at AACJC Forum, 1983.

Louise H. Decker
1 West Conway Street, #1206, Baltimore, MD 21201–2443, (410) 783–4280. b. Baltimore, MD, Feb. 29, 1912. e. Union Memorial Sch. of Nursing, R.N.; TC, B.S., 1941, M.A., 1943.
Employment: instr. in nursing practice, Mountainside Hosp., NJ; educ. dir., Sinai Sch. of Nursing, 1946.

Cleo Kennedy (Heckman) Dell
506 Wintersteen School Road, Millville, PA 17846–0153, (570) 458–6809. b. Millville, PA, Aug. 21, 1919. e. Muncy Valley Private Hosp., L.P.N., 1940; Woman's Med. Coll. of PA, R.N., 1948; TC, B.S., 1959, M.A., 1972.
Employment: dir. of nursing, Danville State Hosp., PA, retired in 1978.

Allan Miles Denton
7 Youngs Lane, Setauket, NY 11733, (631) 941–4583. b. Port Jefferson, NY, July 10, 1932. e. SUNY New Paltz, B.S., 1949–53; TC, M.A., 1953–56.
Employment: elementary sch. instr. and guidance counselor, Three Village Sch. District, NY, 1953–89.

Idilia Reyes de Oliveras
Bailen Street, I–62, Villa Andalucia, San Juan, Puerto Rico 00926.
b. Puerto Rico, Jan. 9, 1914. e. U. of Puerto Rico; NYU; TC, B.S., 1954.
Employment: nursing educ. instr. (10 yrs.); vocational educ. instr.,
Dept. of Educ., San Juan, Puerto Rico (10 yrs.).

John J. Desjarlais
21193 Malta Road, Malta, IL 60150, (815) 825–2086,
jdesjar@kougars.kish.cc.il.us. b. Bad Kreuznach, Germany, March 19,
1953. e. U of Wisconsin-Madison, B.A., 1976; TC, M.A., 1984; Illinois
State Univ., M.A., 1995.

Employment: producer/screenwriter, 2100 Productions, WI,
1984–92; producer, Wisconsin Public Radio, WI, 1992–93; adjunct
English faculty, Illinois Central Coll., IL, 1994; English/
journalism faculty, Kishwaukee Coll., IL, 1995–present.

Publications: 2 books, *The Throne of Tara*, 1990, and *Relics*, 1993;
short fiction, essays, and poetry in *Student Leadership Journal*, *On Being*, *Midwest Writer*, *The Rockford Register Star*, *The Critic*, *The Karitos Review.*

Bonnie Dimun
46 Parsonage Hill Road, Short Hills, NJ 07078, (973) 258–0966,
bdimun@hadassah.org; educ. dir., Hadassah, 50 West 58th Street, New
York, NY 10019. b. Far Rockaway, NY, Nov. 6, 1945. e. Rider U., B.A.,
1967, M.A., 1973; TC, M.A., Ed.D., 1983; Princeton, mid-career fellowship, 1998.

Employment: admin., Middlesex County Coll., 1973–95; educ. dir.,
Hadassah, NY.

Jack H. Dixon
269 Westhampton Drive, Palm Coast, FL 32164, (904) 446–0328,
jackh.dixon@worldnet.att.net; prof., Daytona Beach CC, 1200 International Speedway Boulevard, Daytona Beach, FL 32114. b. Jamaica,
W.I., May 28, 1937. e. Moorhead State, MN, B.S., 1966; CUNY City
Coll., M.S., 1972; TC, M.A., 1982, Ed.D., 1984.

Employment: instr., Malverne Jr. HS, NY, 1966–67; instr., Regional
Opportunity Center, CUNY, 1967–69; educ. dir., Regional Opportunity

Center, CUNY, 1970–72; lecturer, CUNY, acad. skills. dept., 1972–77; principal, Wagner Youth & Adult Center, NY, 1974–76; educ. admin., Manpower Development Training Program, NY, 1976–82; dir., curriculum development unit, Office of Career and Occupational Educ., NY, 1982–83; dir., data collection unit, Office of Occupational Educ., 1983–90; adjunct prof., Borough of Manhattan CC, 1986–90; principal/access dir., Brooklyn Adult Learning Center, 1990–95; adjunct faculty, Daytona Beach CC, 1996–present.

Kevin J. Dougherty
405 Grant Avenue, Highland Park, NJ 08904, (212) 678–8107, kd109@columbia.edu; e. Washington University, B.A., 1972; Harvard, Ph.D. Sociology, 1983.
Employment: assoc. prof. of Higher Education in the Department of Organization and Leadership and senior assoc. at the Community College Research Center, TC, Columbia University.
Publications: The Contradictory College: The Conflicting Origins, Impacts and Futures of the Community College, 1994; "The New Economic Role of the Community College," a CCRC report, 1999; "Community Colleges and Contract Training," *Teachers College Record*, February 2000.

Celeste A. (Lombardi) Dye
270 Bridge Street, R-B 1-1, Bigfork, MT 59911; prof. and dir. M.I.N.T. Project, Montana State U., Bozeman. b. Brooklyn, NY, Jan. 16, 1936. e. Good Samaritan Hosp. Sch. of Nursing, 1957; U. of Maryland, B.S., 1966; TC, M.A., 1967; USC, M.S.Ed., 1969; Purdue, Ph.D., 1972.
Employment: prof., UC San Francisco, 1972–81; asst. prof., Purdue U., 1969–72; assoc. prof., U. of Texas, Austin, 1981–83; prof., SUNY Stony Brook, 1983–2001.
Publications: two textbooks and numerous book chapters and research articles.

Ellen G. Ehrlich
22 Faesch Court, Rockaway, NJ 07866, (973) 328–1065, eerlich@liza.st-elizabeth.edu; assoc. prof., College of St. Elizabeth, 2 Convent Road, Morristown, NJ 07960. b. Detroit, MI, July 17, 1942. e.

Johns Hopkins Hosp. Sch. of Nursing, MD, 1963; Kean Coll., NJ, B.S.N., 1986; TC, M.A., 1988, M.Ed., 1989, Ed.D., 1992.

Employment: asst. supervisor, Mt. Sinai Medical Center, NY, 1963–66; asst. instr., Hosp. of UPenn Sch. of Nursing, 1966–76; admin. and instr., NJ State Dept. of Health EMTs, 1967–75; Lamaze instr., Childbirth Preparation Assoc., MI, 1978–80; staff nurse, St. Barnabas Medical Center, NJ, 1981–94; dir. professional services, Visiting Nurse Service of Morris County, NJ, 1988–90; adjunct prof., Kean Coll., NJ, 1989; asst. prof., Coll. of Mt. St. Vincent, NY, 1990–94; staff nurse, Montefiore Home Health Agency, NY, 1992–93; staff nurse, Northwest Covenant Medical Center, NJ, 1992–98; on-site faculty admin., U. of Medicine and Dentistry of NJ, 1994–2000; assoc. prof., Middlesex County Coll., NJ, 1997–2000; assoc. prof., College of St. Elizabeth, NJ, 2000–present.

Publications: "How We Have Grown," *Focus*, 1992; "On the Road to Self-Discovery: Women's Experience in Psychotherapy," in *In a Woman's Experience*, P. L. Munhall, ed., 1995; "The Holocaust Revisited: Protecting Our Families in the 21st Century," in *The Emergence of the 21st Century Family*, P. L. Munhall, ed., 2001.

J. Judith (Lathrop) Eifert
3202 3rd Street SW, Calgary, AB, Canada T2S1V3, (403) 287–2455, jeifert@mtroyal.ab.ca; VP academics, Mt. Royal Coll., 4825 Richard Road SW, Calgary, AB, Canada, T3E6K6. b. Edmonton, AB, Canada, July 29, 1946. e. U. of Alberta Hosp., 1968; U. of Alberta, B.Sc., 1969; Columbia, M.A., 1979, M.Ed., 1987, Ed.D., 1990.

Employment: Mt. Royal College, nursing instr., 1973–76; chair, allied health dept., 1976–81; special asst. to VP and academic acting dean, 1981; dean, faculty of community and health studies, 1981–82; dean, faculty of continuing educ. and extension, 1982–90; VP, academics, 1990–present; member, Assoc. of Canadian Community Colleges.

Mary-Jane Eisen
50 Ranger Lane, West Hartford, CT 06117, (860) 236–5548, mjeisen@aol.com. e. SUNY Binghamton, B.A., 1973; St. Joseph Coll., M.A., 1991; TC, Ed.D., 1999.

Employment: mobility and recruitment supervisor, Manufacturers Hanover Trust, NY, 1973–78; training services mgr., First Connecticut Bancorp, CT, 1977–78; second VP, personnel services mgr., Covenant Insurance Co., CT, 1973–77; dir. corp. affairs, CDC Fin. Corp., CT, 1988–90; asst. dir., elderhostel, St. Joseph Coll., CT, 1991; designer/trainer, Connecticut Women's Educ. and Legal Fund, 1992–94; consultant, United Way, CT, 1992–96; conference planner, Capital Community Technical Coll., CT, 1992–96; conference planner, Connecticut Permanent Commission on the Status of Women, CT, 1994–95; designer/trainer, NYC Department on Aging, 1995; designer/trainer, Capitol Region Educ. Council, CT, 1995 and 1997; dir., Workforce Development, CT, 2000; adjunct faculty, MCP Hahnemann/Drexel U., PA, 2000; adjunct faculty, American International College, MA, 1994–present; adjunct faculty, U. of Hartford, 1994–present; adjunct faculty, Institute in Gerontology at St. Joseph College, CT, 1995–present.

Publications: "Current Practice and Innovative Programs in Older Adult Learning," *Using Learning to Meet the Challenges of Older Adulthood*, J. C. Fisher and M. A. Wolf, eds., 1998; "Peer Learning Partnerships: Promoting Reflective Practice Through Reciprocal Learning," *Inquiry*, 2000; "Team Teaching and Learning in Adult Education," *New Directions for Adult and Continuing Education*, with E. J. Tisdell, ed., 2000.

Gary L. Eith
8405 Bridlehurst Terrace, Kirtland, OH 44094, (440) 256–8034, home: geith95810@aol.com, work: geith@lakeland.cc.oh.us; dean, community educ., Lakeland CC, 7700 Clocktower Drive, Kirtland, OH 44094. b. Covington, KY, Apr. 21, 1954. e. N. Kentucky U., B.A., 1976; U. of Cincinnati, M.P.A., 1984; TC, Ph.D., 2000.

Employment: N. Kentucky U., asst. to VP for admin. affairs, 1976–81, dir. residential life, 1981–83, adult student services coord., 1983–86, dir. community educ. and service, 1986–89; dean, community educ. division, Lakeland CC, OH, 1991–present.

Publications: "Internationalizing Curriculum," *ERIC*, 2001.

Natividad L. Espiritu
119 DeHaven Drive, #136, Yonkers, NY 10703, (914) 963–3054. b. Caloocan, Rizal, Philippines, Dec. 25, 1934. e. Philippines General

Hosp. Sch. of Nursing, U. of the Philippines, 1956; Philippine Women's U., B.S., 1960, M.A., 1966; TC, M.E., 1978.

Employment: senior faculty, Philippine Women's U., 1964–70; nursing instr., Harlem Hosp. Sch. of Nursing, 1972–73; nursing instr., Mt. Vernon Hosp. Sch. of Nursing, 1973–74; asst. prof., Pace U., 1974–79; adjunct faculty, Borough of Manhattan CC, 1993–94; assoc. prof. and course coord., Helene Fuld Coll. of Nursing, 1985–01.

Publications: "A Report on the Fifth Regional Seminar on Nursing," *The Philippine Journal of Nursing*, 1969; *The Philwomenian Nightingale*, 1969.

Florence Falk-Dickler
1321 Trafalgar Street, Teaneck, NJ 07666, (201) 836–9454, ffalkd@aol.com. b. Brooklyn, NY, July 7, 1931. e. Cornell, 1948–50; U. of Michigan, B.A., 1950–52; NYU, 1952–54; CUNY Brooklyn Coll., M.S., 1962; TC, Ed.D., 1981.

Employment: classroom teacher, 1962–66; high-school counselor/social worker and member of child study team, 1966–71; adult advisor, Bergen CC, NJ, 1971–75; asst. regional admin., U.S. Department of Labor, Women's Bureau, 1975–99.

Jean C. (Barrett) Fayle
18 Corwin Boulevard, Cambridge, Ontario, Canada N1S3L3, (519) 623–0323, jeanfayle@golden.net. b. Niagara Falls, Ontario, Canada, Jan. 12, 1930. e. Galt Collegiate Institute, 1948; Toronto E. General Hosp. Sch. of Nursing, 1951; TC, B.S., 1959.

Employment: health care aide instr., Conestoga Coll., Cambridge Campus, Ontario, 1980–84.

Carol Solon Feldman
23 Blue Ribbon Drive, Westport, CT 06880, (203) 226–6068, csolon@juno.com; prof. of English and humanities, Norwalk CC, 188 Richards Avenue, Norwalk, CT 06850. b. New York, NY, Nov. 25, 1938. e. Queens Coll., B.A., 1960; U. of Bridgeport, M.S., 1972; TC, M.Ed. and Ed.D., 1991.

Employment: reading specialist, NYC public schools, 1960–63; pres., Fairfield County Chapter International Reading Assoc.,

1974–76; consultant, Fairfield County Schools, 1974–80; high sch. English intstructor, 1976–78; prof. of English and the humanities, Norwalk CC, 1978–present; adjunct prof., language studies, Manhattanville Coll., 1996–present; received Educational Excellence and Distinguished Service Award from Norwalk Community–Technical Colleges of Connecticut; awarded a Melon Foundation grant from Yale U., 1997.

Publications: "Journal of Reading," 1980; several articles in *Biz* magazine, 1983–85.

R. Rodney Fields
32 Cavan Drive, Lutherville, MD 21093–5401. b. Palo Alto, CA, June 16, 1938. e. Cornell, B.A.; U. of Baltimore, M.A.; TC, M.A., 1963, Ed.D., 1971.

Employment: nineteen years as provost and dean of faculty at CC of Baltimore, developed allied health, technology, and business programs; twelve years as provost and VP for academic and student affairs at Baltimore International Coll., developed first bachelor's programs and achieved regional, four-year accreditation.

Donald Fitzgerald
349 Norton Hill Road, Ashfield, MA 01330, (413) 628–3349. b. Greenfield, MA, April 4, 1922. e. Oberlin Coll., B.A., 1949; U of Vermont, M.Ed., 1950; TC, Ed.D., 1965.

Employment: ensign, U.S. Navy, 1944–45; Utica CC, 1965–67; U of Mass., 1967–70; Spfd. Tech. CC, 1970–88.

Publications: dissertation, "Review of Massachusetts Community College Needs," 1969; "Accreditation Review," *Spfd. Technical Community College*, 1971.

Henry S. Flax
60 Plaza Street East, Apartment 6K, Brooklyn, NY 11238–5033, (718) 230–8444, hflax@downstate.edu; assoc. dean of student affairs, SUNY Downstate Medical Center, 450 Clarkson Avenue, Box 85, Brooklyn, NY 11203. b. Brooklyn, NY, July 6, 1950. e. Harpur Coll., B.A., 1971; TC, M.A., 1972, Ed.D., 1996; Rutgers, Certified Public Mgr., 1984.

Employment: twenty-nine years in field of educ.

Publications: From Community College to College Community: Transfer Counselors and the Community College Transfer Opportunity Program, 1996.

Betty L. Forest

80 Salisbury Street, Worcester, MA 01609, (508) 755–9495; prof. of nursing emerita, Quinsigamond CC, 670 West Boylston Street, Worcester, MA, 01606. b. New York, NY, July 10, 1932. e. Adelphi, B.S., 1947; TC, M.A., 1957, Ed.D., 1965.

Employment: nursing instr., CUNY Queens Coll., 1957–62; Quinsigamond CC, chair and prof., dept. of nursing, 1965–90, prof. emerita, 1990–present.

Publications: The Utilization of Associate Degree Nursing Graduates in General Hospitals, 1968; "The Utilization of Technical Nurses," in *Technical Nursing, Dimensions and Dynamics*, S. Rasmussen, ed., 1972.

Marie Louise Franciscus

19235 Meadowbrook Court, Fort Myers, FL 33903–6642, (941) 731–1602; prof. emerita, Occupational Therapy Program, College Physicians and Surgeons, Columbia U., 710 West 168th Street, 8th Floor, New York, NY 10032, (212) 305–3781. e. The Grier Sch., PA, 1934; The Philadelphia Sch. of Occupational Therapy, 1937; Ohio State, B.S., 1947; TC, M.A., 1956, Professional Diploma, 1962.

Employment: staff occupational therapist, Pilgrim State Hosp., NY, 1937–41; staff occupational therapist, Children's Rehabilitation Institute, MD, 1941–42; sr. occupational therapist, NY State Rehabilitation Hosp., 1942–44; chief occupational therapist, Crile General Hosp., OH, 1944–46; Occupational Therapy Program, College Physicians and Surgeons, Columbia U., assoc. dir., 1947–48, acting dir., 1948–52, asst. prof. and dir., 1952–59, assoc. prof. and dir., 1959–73, prof. and dir., 1973–81, prof. emerita, 1981–present.

Publications: "The Cerebral Palsied as a Person," *Cerebral Palsy Review*, 1952; "Education of Occupational Therapists in the United States," *The Kinetic Therapy Journal*, 1957; "Occupational Therapy," *World Book Encyclopedia*, 1963.

Dolores Scorca Frank
166–25 Powells Cove Boulevard, Beechhurst, NY 11357, (718) 767–8985; asst. prof., Bronx CC, 181st Street and University Avenue, Bronx, NY 10453. b. New York, NY, Aug. 19, 1936. e. TC, B.S., 1963, Ed.M., 1967.
Employment: asst. prof., Bronx CC, 1967–91.

Barry Freeman
28 Westerly Road, Saddle River, NJ 07458, (201) 825–2094, b-free@att.net; assoc. prof., Bergen CC, 400 Paramus Road, Paramus, NJ 07652, (201) 447–7189. e. U. of Vermont, B.S., 1964; CUNY, M.B.A., 1966; TC, Ed.M., 1993, Ed.D., 1994.
Employment: adjunct asst. prof., U. of Kentucky, 1966–68; research project dir., Ogilvy & Mather Advertising Agency, 1968–70; product mgr., Best Foods, 1970–75; product mgr., Lehn & Fink, 1975–78; adjunct assoc. prof., Pace U., 1976–83; product mgr., Thomas J. Lipton, 1978–83; marketing dir., Good Humor-Breyers Ice Cream Co., 1983–88; owner, Barry Freeman Marketing Consulting, 1988–present; assoc. prof., Bergen CC, 1988–present.

Ruth Dinitz Galligan
75 Sawmill Brook Lane, Mansfield Center, CT 06250, (860) 423–4704. b. New York, NY, July 31, 1927. e. Hunter Coll., B.S., 1954; TC, M.A., 1955.
Employment: instr., Queens Coll., 1955–56, established psychiatric nursing curriculum; instr., Mohegan CC, CT, 1974–87, also established psychiatric nursing curriculum at this institution; instr., Norwich State Hosp.

Edna Gardenier
207 Holsapple Road, Dover Plains, NY 12552, (845) 877–3345, ehgarden@earthlink.net. b. Teaneck, NJ, June 30, 1935. e. Newark Beth Israel Hosp. Sch. of Nursing, 1952–55; Seton Hall, 1956–65; TC, M.Ed., 1967–70; SUNY Albany, Ed.D., 1990.
Employment: nursing instr., East Orange General and Englewood Hosps., 1955–65; Dutchess County Health Department, staff nurse/supervisor, 1965–70, instr., Assoc. Degree Nursing Prog.,

1970–71, acting prog. chair, 1971–72, prog. chair, 1972–80, asst. to the pres., 1980–81, dept. head of health technologies, 1981–82, dept. head of nursing, 1982–99; faculty member, Regents College Nursing Programs, 1980–92.

Publications: dissertation, *The Transformation from the Hospital School to the Community Junior College: A Step Toward the Professionalization of Nursing (1873–1965).*

Maureen Mulholland Garretson
2561 Tamalpais Avenue, El Cerrito, CA 94530, (510) 236–4115; instr., Contra Costa Coll., Mission Bell Drive, San Pablo, CA 94806. b. New York, NY, Nov. 9, 1934. e. Coll. of Mt. St. Vincent, B.S., 1956; TC, M.A., 1959.

Employment: instr., Brooklyn Coll., 1959–60; San Francisco State U., 1960–62; Coll. of Marin, 1969–70; Northeastern U., 1970–71; UC San Francisco, 1971–72; U. of San Francisco, 1972–73; Hayward State U., 1973–74; Contra Costa Coll., 1974–present.

Rosalyn M. Ghysels
3545 Whispering Brook Drive SE, Kentwood, MI 49508–3733, (616) 475–4677, rghysels@ionline.com; dir. practical nursing, chair, health division, and instr., Grand Rapids CC, 143 Bostwick NE, Grand Rapids, MI 49503. b. Grand Rapids, MI, Oct. 11, 1926. e. Johns Hopkins, B.S.N., 1953; TC, M.A., 1960.

Employment: instr., Blodgett Hosp. Sch. of Nursing, 1954–59; Grand Rapids CC, dir, practical nursing, 1959–67, chair, health div., 1963–67, instr., assoc. degree nursing, 1967–91.

Michael C. Gillespie
345 East 93rd Street, #3F, New York, NY 10128, (212) 410–9235, DrMCG7@aol.com. b. Mount Vernon, New York, June 10, 1950. Associate Dean of Academic Affairs, Borough of Manhattan Community College, 199 Chambers Street, New York, NY 10027. e. Brown University, A.B.–M.A.T., 1972; Teachers College, M.A., 1980; Teachers College, Ed.D., 1983.

Employment: presently assoc. dean of academic affairs, Borough of Manhattan CC; prof. and coord. of Teacher Education, sen. dir. of collaborative programs, dir. of Bronx Education Alliance, Bronx CC, Danforth foundation assoc., 1992–2001; dir. of Manhattan and Bronx Principals' Centers, City College of New York, Danforth foundation assoc., 1987–92; educ. and personnel officer, Manufacturers Hanover Trust, NY, 1980–87; adjunct instr. of English and Humanities, Marymount Manhattan College, NY, & American Institute of Banking, NY, 1978–80; English teacher, Classical HS, Providence, RI, 1972–78; English teacher, Phillips Academy, Andover, MA, 1971–75.

Publications: "Shared Decision-Making as Enduring Process," *Journal of NYC ASCD*, 1990; "Bronx Educational Alliance: Working for Permanent Change," *Alliance*, 1995; "'Fridays at the College' Has Created an Urban Learning Environment," *Middle School Journal*, 1997; "An Urban Intervention that Works: The Bronx Corridor of Success," *Creating and Benefiting from Institutional Collaboration*, 1998.

Wilhelmina B. Glanville
626 Riverside Drive, #17A, New York, NY 10031–7224, (212) 862–6819. b. New York, NY, Dec. 21, 1925. e. Harlem Hosp. Sch. of Nursing, 1953–56; TC, B.S., 1957–60, M.A., 1962, Ed.M., 1981, Ed.D., 1989.

Employment: head nurse, clinical instr., Harlem Hosp. Sch. of Nursing, 1957–63; federally funded Manpower Development Training Program for Practical Nurses, NYC Board of Educ., nursing instr., 1963–66, asst. dir., 1966–71; BMCC, CUNY, asst. prof. and deputy chair, nursing, 1973–79, assoc. prof. and chair, nursing, 1979–88, prof., 1985–93, prof. emerita, 1993–present.

Publications: dissertation, *An Involvement Program to Increase Retention of Remedial Pre-Nursing Students in a Clinical Nursing Program: Implications for Public Urban Community College Educators*, 1989.

Marjorie Kiselik Glusker
21 Larchmont Street, Ardsley, NY 10502, (914) 693–2297, marge.glusker@sunywcc.edu; dean of continuing educ., Westchester CC, 75 Grasslands Road, Valhalla, NY 10595, (914) 785–6585. b. Newark, NJ, June 19, 1944. e. Columbia, B.A., 1966; Queens Coll., M.S., 1968; TC, M.A., 1983, Ed.D., 1983.

Employment: Dept. of Health, Educ., and Welfare, Washington, DC, 1966–71; instr., Bureau of Fundamental Adult Educ., NYC Board of Educ., 1971–74; consultant in higher educ., business, and government, 1974–present; Cornell U., NY State Sch. of Industrial and Labor Relations, project coord., 1979–80, program dir., 1980–82, district dir., 1983–89; Westchester CC, asst. dean, div. of continuing educ., 1989–92, assoc. dean, 1992–95, dean, 1995–present.

Publications: "Westchester Community College: Marketing to Special Populations," *The College Board: Demographics Shape the Future of Higher Education*, 2000.

Charlotte Brown Greever
152 Crawfish Road, Rural Retreat, VA 24368, (540) 686–4929. b. Monroe, NC, Dec. 2, 1913. e. UNC Greensboro, A.B., 1935; TC, M.A., 1950; additional summer study at UVA.

Employment: high-school instr., NC, 1935–48; guidance counselor, VA, 1949–77; p/t psychology instr., Myrtle County CC, 1965.

Publications: two articles about local church and community in the *Myrtle County Historical Review*, 1972 and 1974.

Adele J. Gurda
4 Randall Heights, Middletown, NY 10940, (845) 343–5445. b. New York, NY, Apr. 2, 1918. e. Middletown State Hosp., 1939; TC, B.S., 1960, M.A., 1963.

Employment: assoc. prof., Orange County CC, 1960–73.

Minerva S. Guttman
16 Trails End Court, Westfield, NJ 07091, (908) 789–0099, guttman@mailbox.fdu.edu; dir., Sch. of Nursing and Allied Health, Fairleigh Dickinson U., 1000 River Road, HDH4–02, Teaneck, NJ 07666. b. Philippines, June 29, 1946. e. U. of the Philippines, B.S.N., 1968; TC, M.A., 1977, M.Ed., 1991, Ed.D., 1992; postmaster's certificate, nurse practitioner, U. of Medicine and Dentistry of NJ.

Employment: instr., U. of the Philippines, Philippine Gen. Hosp. Sch. of Nursing, 1969–73; instr., Beth Israel Sch. of Nursing, 1974–79; asst. prof., SUNY, 1979–93; U. of Medicine and Dentistry of NJ, Middlesex CC Joint ASN Program, chair and assoc. prof.,

1993–96, asst. dean and assoc. prof., 1996–99; dir. and assoc. prof., Fairleigh Dickinson U., 1999–present.

David L. Hadaller
290 West 232nd Street, Bronx, NY 10463, dlhadallernyc@juno.com; asst. dean of academic affairs, Hostos CC, CUNY, 500 Grand Concourse, Room B464, Bronx, NY 10451, (718) 518–6725. e. Gonzaga U., B.A., 1976; St. Louis U., M.A., 1979; Washington State, Ph.D., 1993; Columbia, M.A., 1999.
Employment: Hostos CC, coord. of special projects, 1996–98, asst. dean of academic affairs, 1998–present, chair of the language and cognition department, 1999, acting chief librarian, 2000–01.

James F. Hall
29 Liverpool Drive, Yarmouth Port, MA 02675–1526, (508) 362–2471, hallo@cape.com. e. U of Michigan, 1939–41; Wayne State Univ., B.A., 1941–42, M.Ed., 1946–48; TC, Ed.D, 1953.

Joseph N. Hankin
4 Merion Drive, Purchase, NY 10577, (914) 761–0038, joseph.hankin@ sunywcc.edu; pres., Westchester CC, 75 Grasslands Road, Valhalla, NY 10595. b. New York, NY, Apr. 6, 1940. e. CCNY, B.A., 1961; Columbia, M.A., 1962; TC, Ed.D., 1967; doctor of letters, honoris causa, Mercy Coll., 1979; doctor of humane letters, honoris causa, Coll. of New Rochelle, 1996; doctor of pedagogy, honoris causa, Manhattan Coll., 2000.
Employment: CCNY, fellow, 1962–63, lecturer, 1963–65; lecturer, Brooklyn Coll., 1963; lecturer, Queens Coll., 1964; TC, course asst., 1965, ongoing lecturer, 1965–present, adjunct prof. and visiting prof., 1976; Harford Jr. Coll., dir. of evening division and summer session, 1965–66, dean of continuing educ. and summer session, 1966–67, pres. 1967–71; pres., Westchester CC, 1971–present.
Publications: The Community Junior College: An Annotated Bibliography, Emory Rarig, ed., 1966; "The Door that Never Closes," *Community and Junior College Journal*, 1973; "Assessing Quality Excellence and Honesty," in *Students and Their Institutions: A Changing Relationship*, J. W. Peltason and Marcy V. Massengale, eds., 1978; "Community Colleges Offer Multiple Choices," *School Guide College*

Conference Manual, 1983; "A Community College Means Business," *Westchester Business Journal*, 1983; "What Makes the Community College Distinctive," in *A Search for Institutional Distinctiveness*, Barbara K. Townsend, ed., 1989; "Community Colleges and the Information Age," *Community, Technical, and Junior College Journal*, 1991; "Academic Scruples: Faculty and Personnel Issues," in *Dilemmas of Leadership: Decision Making and Ethics in the Community College*, George B. Vaughan, et al., 1992; "Literature a Community College President Should Read to be More Effective," *Community College Journal of Research and Practice*, 1993; *Community Colleges: Opportunities and Access for America's First-Year Students*, with John N. Gardner, Betsy O. Barefoot, and Dorothy S. Fidler, eds., 1996.

Phyllis Walton Haring
2533 West Lake Drive, Deland, FL 32724, (386) 738–1988; prof. emeritus, Nassau CC, Garden City, NY, 11530. b. Richmond, VA, Jan. 21, 1923. e. Queens Coll., A.A.S., 1958; Adelphi, NY, B.S., 1961, M.S., 1964; Columbia, M.S., 1970, Ed.D., 1975.

Employment: instr., nursing, Adelphi U., NY, 1961–64; prof., nursing, Nassau CC, NY, 1964–85; adjunct prof., nursing, Daytona CC, FL, 1985–98.

Publications: Care of Patients with Emotional Problems, with Dolores Saxton, 1971; "Short-Term Adjustment of Geriatric Residents," *Mental Health Nursing*, 1978.

Josephine Mary Harrison
14 Crownwood Lane, Queensbury, NY 12804, (518) 793–3530. b. New York, NY, Mar. 19, 1923. e. Queens Coll., A.A.S., 1955–57; TC, B.S.N., 1964, M.A., 1968, postmaster's coursework.

Employment: operating room nurse, Long Island Jewish Medical Center, 1957–61; public health nurse, Nassau County Dept. of Health, 1961–64; nursing instr., Adirondack CC, 1964–83.

Joanne L. Heinly
214 Walnut Street, Lebanon, PA 17042, (717) 273–7832, joloh@nbn.net. b. Allentown, PA, June 4, 1932. e. Susquehanna U., 1950–52; Columbia U. Sch. of Nursing, 1952–55; TC, M.A., 1964.

Employment: instr., Columbia U. Sch. of Nursing, 1961–64; instr., U. of Illinois Coll. of Nursing, 1964–66; assoc. prof., William Rainey Harper Coll., 1966–89 (established assoc. degree nursing program and designed the continuing educ. program).

Publications: "The Patient's Need for Recreation," *Current Concepts in Clinical Nursing*, Betty S. Bergersen, et al., 1967.

Sister Grace Henke

130 West 12th Street, New York, NY 10011, (212) 604–8488, ghenke@saintvincentsnyc.org; ethics assoc., St. Vincent's Hosp. and Medical Center, 130 West 12th Street, New York, NY 10011. b. New York, NY, Feb. 24, 1932. e. St. Vincent's Hosp. Sch. of Nursing, 1957; Hunter, B.S., 1962, M.S., 1964; TC, Ed.D., 1978; certification, long-term care ombudsman, NY State Office for Aging, 1999; certification in human subjects research training, Johns Hopkins, MD, 2000.

Employment: instr., St. Vincent's Hosp. Sch. of Nursing, 1962–98; adjunct prof., College of Mt. St. Vincent, 1982–present.

Publications: Med-Math: Dosage Calculation, Preparation, and Administration, 1991; co-author, *Stepping Stones to Success: Study Skills for Student Nurses*, 1992.

Dorothy M. Hibbert

1201 Richmond Street, #215, London, Ontario, Canada N6A3L6, (519) 438–2788, d.hibbert@sympatico.ca. b. Boissevain, Manitoba, Canada, Jan. 18, 1915. e. Winnipeg Gen. Hosp., nursing diploma, 1937; U. of Manitoba, 1943–44; TC, B.S., 1953, M.A., 1957, professional diploma, 1958.

Employment: surgical teaching in nursing, 1948–50; asst. dir. of nursing, 1950–57; asst. prof., U. of Saskatchewan, 1958–63; visiting prof., U. of New Brunswick, 1961–62; U. of W. Ontario, assoc. prof., 1963–68; prof., 1968; asst. dean, nursing, 1969; acting dean, nursing, 1977–78; 1980–present, prof. emerita.

Mildred B. Hoff

16 Lindbergh Place, Poughkeepsie, NY 12603, (845) 454–0623, dottieho@juno.com; prof. emerita, Dutchess CC, Pendell Road, Poughkeepsie, NY 12603. b. New York, NY, June 13, 1917. e. Hudson River State Hosp. Sch. of Nursing, 1939; TC, B.S., 1960, M.A., 1962.

Employment: nursing instr., 1942–46; asst. principal, Sch. of Nursing, Central Islip State Hosp., 1947–49; Sch. of Nursing, Hudson River State Hosp., instr., 1950–52, asst. principal, 1957–61, principal, 1961–63; Dutchess CC, asst. prof., 1963–73, assoc. prof., 1974–78, prof. emerita, 1978–present.

Katherine Houghton-Zatz
146 Cherry Lane, Teaneck, NJ 07666, (201) 836–0744, drkzatz@ yahoo.com; dean of student affairs and adjunct faculty, Hudson County CC, 162 Sip Avenue, Jersey City, NJ 07306, (201) 714–7888. b. Iron Mountain, MI, Oct. 28, 1959. e. U. of Wisconsin, 1978–80; Macalester, MN, B.A., 1982; TC, M.A., 1985, M.Ed., 1991, Ed.D., 1993; Harvard, Institute for Educ. Management, 1999; Wellesley, Higher Educ. Research Services, 2000–01.

Employment: student hall dir., Macalester Coll., 1981; residence hall dir. and counselor, Hubert H. Humphrey Job Corps Center, MN, 1982–84; campus activities dir., Mundelein Coll, IL, 1985–87; dir. of student development and adjunct faculty, Coll. of St. Francis, IL, 1987–90; dir., specialized housing, Columbia U., 1991–93; dean of student services, Coll. of Aeronautics, NY, 1993–97; dean of student affairs and adjunct faculty, Hudson County CC, NJ, 1997–present.

Publications: "Comparison of Campus Alcohol Policies of Chicago Area Colleges and Universities," *Association of Campus Activities Administrators,* 1989; "Turn Problem Employees into Assets," *Administrator,* 1999.

James Hoyt
135 Lido Boulevard, Lido Beach, NY 11561, (516) 889–5292, hoytj@sunynassau.edu; prof., Nassau CC. b. New York, Apr. 26, 1947. e. Montclair State, B.A., 1965–69; TC, M.A., 1972–73; C.W. Post Center, Long Island U., 1979–82; NYU, Ph.D., 1982–89.

Employment: teacher, U.S. Peace Corps, Malawi, Africa, 1969–71; Nassau CC, counselor, Financial Counseling Center, 1973–76, prof. and transfer counselor, 1977–present, co-chair of the Academic Senate Committee on the College Mission, 1984–85, co-chair of the Academic Senate Committee on Core Curriculum,

1984–86, second vice chair, academic senate, 1987–91 and 1993–97, adjunct instr., 1989–present, member, negotiating team, Federation of Teachers, 1991, member, Middle States Accreditation Steering Committee, 1992; project assoc., National Center for Urban Partnerships, Bronx CC, 1997.

Patricia A. Hyland
69 Princeton Street, Garden City, NY 11530, (516) 352–8658. b. Jamaica, NY, Aug. 8, 1930. e. Coll. of Mt. St. Vincent, B.S.N., 1952; St. John's, NY, M.S., 1957; TC, M.S.Ed., Ed.D., 1978.

Employment: St. Clare's Hosp. Sch. of Nursing, 1957–65; prof., Nassau CC, 1965–90, chair, nursing department, 1968–77, prof. emerita, 1990–present.

Publications: Manual of Nursing Practice, with Saxton, et al., 1983; *Planning and Implementing Nursing Intervention*, with Saxton, 1975; dissertation, *Comparison of Achievement on the Clinical Performance of Nursing Examinations Between Conventional Associate Degree Nursing Students and Candidates for the New York State Regents External Degree Program*, TC, 1978.

Veronica Johnson
3751 Willett Avenue, Bronx, NY 10467, (718) 654–2254. e. Kingston Public Hosp., Jamaica, W.I., nursing diploma, 1968; St. Joseph's Coll., Brooklyn, B.S., 1976; TC, M.Ed., 1980.

Employment: staff nurse, Children's Hosp., Jamaica, W.I., 1968–70; midwife, Lincoln Medical Center, NY, 1970–71; staff nurse, Queens Hosp. Center, NY, 1978–82; Hosp. for Joint Diseases, NY, staff development instr., 1982–87, clinical nurse specialist, 1987–88, professional development coord., 1982–90, clinical instr., 1993–95; adjunct prof., U. of Medicine and Dentistry of NJ, 1984–85; adjunct prof., Long Island U., 1985–86; case mgr., Florida Hosp., 1990–93; visiting nurse service, 1995–2000; adjunct prof., Bronx CC, 1995–2000; adjunct prof., Coll. of New Rochelle, 1995–2000; educ. coord., Kingsbrook Jewish Medical Center, NY, 2000–present.

Publications: "Primary Team Nursing: The 90s Model," *Nursing Management*, 1993.

Arlyne M. Kellock
45–41 39th Place, #1L, Sunnyside, NY 11104, (718) 937–5548; asst. prof., CUNY Kingsborough CC, 2001 Oriental Boulevard, Brooklyn, NY 11235. b. New York, NY, Mar. 31, 1946. e. Fairleigh Dickinson, NJ, B.S.N., 1970; TC, M.A., 1976, Ed.M., 1977.
Employment: St. Clare's Hosp. Sch. of Nursing, 1970–76; Skidmore Coll., 1977–83; Phillips Beth Israel Sch. of Nursing, 1987–96; Kingsborough CC, 1996–present.
Publications: Barron's How to Prepare for the National Council Licensure Examination for Registered Nurses, with Sadie Small and Luzviminda Casapao, 2000.

Jacqueline W. Kineavy
6 Elizabeth Parkway, Eatontown, NJ 07724, (732) 542–3333, jkineavy@pccc.cc.nj.us; VP for academic and student affairs, Passaic County CC, 1 College Boulevard, Paterson, NJ 07505–1179. e. Fairleigh Dickinson, NJ, A.A., nursing, M.A.; UPenn, B.S.N.; Seton Hall, NJ, M.S.N.; TC, Ed.D.
Employment: staff nurse, Monmouth Medical Center, 1967; staff nurse, Riverview Medical Center, NJ, 1967–68; staff nurse, Thomas Jefferson U. Hosp., PA, 1967–70; faculty member, Penn. Hosp. Sch. of Nursing, 1970–72; Ann May Sch. of Nursing, NJ, faculty member, 1972–79 and 1984–85; dir. staff educ., Community Memorial Hosp., NJ, 1980–84; assoc. dir., Jersey Shore Medical Center, 1985–88; adjunct faculty, Seton Hall U., NJ, 1989–2000; Passaic County CC, dir. of nurse educ., 1989–1994, acting dean of faculty, 1990–91, acting exec. asst. to the pres., 1992, assoc. dean for instruction, 1994–97, VP for academic affairs and dean of faculty, 1997–2000, VP for academic and student affairs, 2000–present.

Robert E. Kinsinger
21901 Confidence Road, Twain Harte, CA 95383, (209) 586–4709. b. Chicago, IL, Aug. 5, 1923. e. Stanford, A.B., 1948, M.A., 1951; TC, Ed.D., 1958; honorary degrees received include Thomas Jefferson U., Litt.D., Hahnemann U., L.H.D., Simpson Coll., L.L.D.; received TC Distinguished Alumnus Award, 1981.

Employment: during WWII, officer-in-charge, air/sea rescue, U.S. Navy; staff member, U.S. delegation, 3rd general assembly of the United Nations, Paris, 1948; mgr., American Red Cross Northwest Regional Blood Center; lecturer, Queens Coll. and Columbia U.; educ. consultant, National League for Nursing, 1957–60; admin., Health Careers Project, SUNY, 1960–66; VP, W. K. Kellogg Foundation, 1966–83; member or chairperson of various boards including Jossey-Bass Publishers and Excelsior Coll.

Publications: Education for Health Technicians: An Overview; *Clinical Nursing Instruction by Television*; ed., *Opportunities for Health Technicians.*

Elaine S. Klein
24 Van Meter Fens, New Rochelle, NY 10804, (914) 632–2477. b. New York, NY, Oct. 17, 1928. e. Hunter Coll., NY, 1948, M.A., 1951; TC, Ph.D., 1961.

Employment: faculty, Hunter Coll., NY, 1948–52; Marymount Manhattan Coll., prof. and department chair, 1952–67, [first layperson] academic dean, 1967–72; founding dean, Iona Coll., 1972–74; Westchester CC, [first woman] assoc. dean, 1974–80, faculty, 1980–98.

Sarah W. Korn
13801 York Road, #F5, Cockeysville, MD 21030, (410) 785–8438, swkorn@myseniors.com. b. Camden, NJ, July 9, 1920. e. Penn. Hosp. Sch. of Nursing, 1941; UPenn, B.S.E., 1944; TC, B.A., 1959; Johns Hopkins, M.Ed., 1971.

Employment: Penn. Hosp. Sch. of Nursing, 1944–59; UNC Greensboro, 1960–65; Baltimore Jr. Coll., 1965–66; Catonsville CC, 1966–84.

Alice F. Kucmeroski
5 Lolly Lane, Centereach, NY 11720, (631) 585–7604, a.kucmeroski@verizon.net; assoc. prof., nursing, Suffolk County CC, 533 College Road, Selden, NY 11784–2899. b. Brooklyn, NY, June 7, 1942. e. St. John's Hosp. Sch. of Nursing, NY, 1962; St. John's U., NY, B.S., 1965; TC, M.A., 1976; Southhampton Coll., NY, graduate certificate in gerontology.

Employment: float nurse, St. John's Queens Hosp., 1962–64; float nurse, Hillcrest Gen. Hosp., NY, 1964–65; public health nurse, Suffolk County Department of Health, 1965–70; adjunct instr., nursing, BOCES, NY, 1973–74; St. John's Episcopal Hosp., staff nurse, 1972–76, asst. dir., nursing, 1976–78; adjunct instr., Adelphi U., NY, 1976–78; Suffolk CC, NY, adjunct instr., 1979–80 and 1994; John T. Mather Memorial Hosp., NY, nursing coord., 1978–81, asst. VP for nursing educ., 1981–94; Able Home Care Co., NY, nursing coord., 1994, nurse mgr., 1994–95; home care nurse, Nursing Sisters Home Visiting Service, NY, 1995–98; Suffolk CC, NY, instr., medical and surgical nursing, 1995–97, asst. prof., 1997–2001, assoc. prof., 2001–present.

Shawn Ladda
3215 Netherland Avenue, #5A, Bronx, NY 10463, (718) 601–2013, sladda@manhattan.edu; asst. prof. and chair, Manhattan Coll., Department of Physical Education and Human Performance, Bronx, NY 10471, (718) 862–7811. b. Chicago, IL, June 30, 1961. e. Penn State, B.S., 1983; Springfield Coll., MA, M.S., 1985; TC, Ed.M., 1993, Ed.D., 1995.

Employment: teacher and coach at various soccer camps, 1981–present; Springfield Coll., asst. women's soccer coach and phys. educ. instr., 1983–84, athletic admin. field work, 1984; girl's basketball and tennis coach, full-time substitute teacher, Weston HS, MA, 1985–86; women's soccer, basketball, and lacrosse coach, phys. educ. instr., admin. asst., M.I.T., 1985–88; women's soccer coach and phys. educ. assoc., Columbia U., 1988–94; asst. prof. of phys. educ. and human performance, Manhattan Coll., 1994–present.

Publications: "Reflections of the World Cup," *Soccer Journal*, 1992; "Ornamental and Useless? Women's Involvement with Soccer was Part of the Emancipation Process," *Soccer Journal*, 1999; "The Early Beginnings of Intercollegiate Women's Soccer," *The Physical Educator*, 2000.

Lois Lagerman
28 Meadow Lane, Glen Head, NY 11545, (516) 671–2553, llagerman@aol.com; asst. prof., nursing, Borough of Manhattan CC,

199 Chambers Street, New York, NY 10007. b. New York, NY, Apr. 17, 1939. e. Kings County Hosp. Sch. of Nursing, 1964; Brooklyn Coll., B.S., 1974; Hunter Coll., M.S.N., B.S.N., 1981; TC, Ed.D., 1996; Adelphi, NY, nurse practitioner certificate, 1997.

Employment: special procedure nurse, Methodist Hosp., NY, 1973–82; dir. staff educ., Gracie Square Hosp., 1982–84; faculty advisor, Adelphi, NY, 1990–91; staffing coord., Booth Memorial Medical Center, NY, 1990–93; asst. prof., Iona Coll., NY, 1992–94; supervision, nursing educ. and dir., ambulatory care, Hempstead Gen. Hosp., 1992–95; adjunct teaching, Farmingdale CC, 1995; adjunct teaching, Suffolk CC, 1996; outpatient clinic, Fort Hamilton Army Base, 1987–91; nurse practitioner, Inter Nutritional Network, 1996–present; medical and surgical nursing, North Shore Hosp., 1994–98; critical care instr., UPenn at NYU Medical Center, 1997–present; asst. prof. nursing, BMCC, 1998–present.

Publications: "Jacqueline Hott, Ph.D.," *Nursing Leader*; *American Nursing: A Biographical Dictionary*, vol. 3, 2000.

Yolanda C. Landrau
12 Johnson Street, Falmouth, MA 02540, (508) 457–4202; ylandrau@ capecod.net. b. New York, NY, Aug. 24, 1935. e. Hunter Coll., B.S.N., 1969, M.S.N., 1971; TC, Ed.D., 1985.

Employment: staff nurse, Newark Beth Israel Medical Center, NJ, 1958–60; supervisor, Monroe-Jackson Hosp., FL, 1960–61; supervisor, maternity, Mt. Sinai Hosp., NY, 1961–65; asst. prof., Bronx CC, CUNY, 1971–78; adjunct prof., Pace U., NY, 1972–79; special asst., St. John's Episcopal Hosp., NY; dir., URC Associates, 1974–85; mgr./asst. dir., nursing, the Hosp. Assoc. of NY State, 1979–82; VP, nursing, Bridgeport Hosp., CT, 1982–86; adjunct prof., Massachusetts Bay CC, 1986–96; Neponset Valley Health System, VP for patient care services, 1986–91, SVP for patient care and behavioral medicine, 1991–92, exec. VP operations, 1992–95, pres. and CEO, 1995–98; consultant, Caritas Christi Health Care System, 1998–present.

Publications: dissertation, *Nurses' Attitudes and Their Ability to Identify Alcoholism in a Patient Situation*, 1985.

Robert Reid Lawrence

2143 Alta Avenue, Louisville, KY 40205, (502) 456–6013, Robert.Lawrence@kctcs.net, BOBSYRL@aol.com; assoc. prof., Jefferson CC, 109 East Broadway, Louisville, KY 40202. b. Columbus, OH, Nov. 9, 1940. e. U. of Louisville, B.A., 1963; Wagner, NY, M.A., 1966; NYU, M.A., 1970; TC, Ed.D., 1980.

Employment: instr., Louisville public schools, 1963–64; Wagner Coll., teaching asst., 1964–66, English instr., 1966–73; Jefferson CC, KY, English instr. 1976–present, coord. of academic advising, 1987–98, interim division chair, humanities, 1988–99, currently working full-time as an advisor in professional development.

Publications: "'The Mind Alone': History of the Publications and Criticism of the Letters of Emily Dickinson," *Emily Dickinson Bulletin*, Part I, 1970, Part II, 1971, Part III, 1972.

Martin Lecker

15 Woodthrusk Drive, West Nyack, NY 10994–1120, (845) 358–4509, mlecker@sunyrockland.edu; prof. of business and coord. of mgmt. services, Rockland CC, 145 College Road, Suffern, NY 10901. b. Yonkers, NY, February 7, 1950. e. Pace Coll., B.B.A., 1968–72; Pace Univ., M.B.A., 1974–78; TC, Ed.M/Ed.D, 1987–90.

Employment: assistant credit manager, United Factors, NY, 1972–73; customer service rep., Xerox Corp., NY, 1973–74; adjunct assistant prof. of business, SUNY, NY, 1980–81; business instr. and dept. chairperson, Rhinebeck HS, NY, 1974–82; accounting instr., Ridgefield HS, CT, 1982–84; temp. full-time instructor, Rockland CC, NY, 1985–86, assistant prof. of business, Rockland CC, NY, 1986–89; assoc. prof. of business, Rockland CC, NY, 1989–91; chairperson, business dept., Rockland CC, NY, 1991–94; coord., business honors program, Rockland CC, NY, 1990–present; prof. of business, Rockland CC, NY, 1991–present.

Publications: "Psychoethics: A Discipline Applying Psychology to Business Ethics," *Perspectives in Business Ethics, 1998*; *Multicultural Readings in Business and Industry, second edition*, 1998; "Psychoethics: A discipline Applying Psychology to Ethics," *Review of Business*, 1997; "The US Government Reforms Child Product Safety Laws," *Great Events from History II*, 1994; "Nader's Unsafe at Any Speed Launches a

Consumer Mvmnt.," in *Great Events from History II*, 1994; "Integrated Communications Skills on a CC Level," *Colleague*, 1991; "The Market Basket Survey," *Business Exchange*, 1988; "PR Assignment," *Good Writing*, 1988; "Increase your students stock market literacy," *Business Educ. Forum*, 1982; "Learning Accounting Under the Mastery Teaching Technique System," *Business Educ. Forum*, 1982; "Starting Your Own Student Employment Agency," *Today's Secretary*, 1981; "The CPA Game," *Business Exchange*, 1981.

Gloria Leifer
307 West 6th Street, Ontario, CA 91762, (909) 983–8827, leiferhartson@cs.com; assoc. prof., pediatric nursing, Riverside CC, 4800 Magnolia Avenue, Riverside, CA 92506. b. New York, NY, Apr. 10, 1935. e. Fordham Sch. of Nursing, 1955; Hunter Coll., NY, B.S., 1960; TC, M.A., 1962, Ed.D. (incomplete).

Employment: instr., Fordham Sch. of Nursing (3 yrs.); instr., Hunter Coll. nursing department (5 yrs.); asst. prof., California State Coll., LA (1 yr.); assoc. prof., Riverside CC (11 yrs.); pediatric consultant (5 yrs.).

Publications: "Rooming-in Despite Complications Postpartum," *American Journal of Nursing*, 1964; ed., "Symposium on Nurse and Ill Child," *Nursing Clinics of North America*, 1966; *Principles and Techniques in Pediatric Nursing*, 1982; "Less Isn't More if You Can't Read it," *RN*, 1993; "Pediatric Cheat Sheet," *RN*, with M. Brown, 1998; *Introduction to Maternity and Pediatric Nursing*, 1999; *Introduction to Maternity Nursing*, with A. Burroughs, 2000; "Hyperbaric Oxygen Therapy: Nurse's Role," 2001; "Aromatherapy and the Nurse," 2001.

Seyma Louise Ocko Levine
465 Meer Avenue, Wyckoff, NJ 07481, (201) 891–4177. e. Syracuse, B.S.; TC, M.A., Ed.M., Ed.D., 1994.

Employment: "My career in education has been as an educational consultant in business and industry, community development, health-care, and higher education."

Publications: dissertation, *Study Circles: A Mode of Learning for Older Adults in the Community College Setting*, 1994; *Preparing Students for the New World: Service Learning in the Americas and Elsewhere*, 1996.

Winifred P. Lewis

4826 South Greenwood Avenue, Chicago, IL 60615, (773) 373–2041, winnie_lewis@tahitiannoni.com; dir. of nursing, U. of Chicago Hospitals, 6130 North Sheridan Road, Chicago, IL 60660. b. Guyana, South America, July 21, 1954. e. Bronx CC, A.A.S., 1974; Long Island U., B.S.N., 1980; TC, M.A., 1985.

Employment: Memorial Sloan-Kettering Cancer Unit, NY, staff nurse, gynecology, 1974–76, staff nurse, intensive care, 1976–78, nurse mgr., thoracic unit, 1978–83, asst. dir. nursing, 1983–86, dir. nursing, 1986–92, dir. nursing practice, 1992–96; U. of Chicago Hospitals, dir., oncology care center, 1997–98, dir., oncology and general medicine care centers, 1998–present.

Elizabeth Reid Lovell

609 Boyd Mill Avenue, #16, Franklin, TN 37064, (615) 794–3182. b. Madison Co., TN, Aug. 16, 1914. e. Vanderbilt U. Sch. of Nursing, TN, 1936; TC, B.S., 1954.

Employment: public health nurse (retired).

Judith W. Lowin

20 Sands Point Road, Monsey, NY 10952–2113, (845) 352–4917, judylowin@aol.com; assoc. prof., nursing and curriculum chair, ADN prog., Westchester CC, 75 Grasslands Road, Valhalla, NY 10595. b. New York, NY, Aug. 7, 1943. e. Hunter Coll., NY, B.S., 1965, TC, M.A., 1977.

Employment: instr., Miami-Dade Jr. Coll., 1970–71; adjunct instr., Rockland CC, 1975–79; instr., Queensborough CC, 1977–78; Westchester CC, 1979–present.

Barbara A. Macauley

80 Salisbury Street, #301, Worcester, MA 01609, (508) 756–3112; dir., I-495 Center for Professional Education, UMass, Karl Weiss Education and Conference Center, 100 North Drive, Westborough, MA 01581, (508) 616–7909, macauley@donahue.umassp.edu. e. Springfield, B.S., 1971; Worcester State, M.Ed., 1977; TC, M.A., 1993, Ed.D., 1995.

Employment: social worker, Children's Protective Services, DE, 1971–74; asst. dir, youth group services, YMCA, MA, 1974–77; coord.,

MAGNET educ. program, MA, 1977–78; program development specialist, New England Center for Community Educ., UConn, 1978–80; adult educ. program coord., CT State Dept. of Educ., 1980–81; educ. services specialist, CT State Dept. of Educ., 1981–82; consultant, Department of Youth Services, MA, and research asst., Worcester State Coll., 1982–83; adjunct graduate faculty, Worcester State Coll., 1985–90; Quinsigamond CC, Center for Lifelong Learning, dir. of community services, 1983–86, asst. dean, 1986–90, assoc. dean, 1990–94, assoc. dean of academic affairs, 1994–96, assoc. dean, continuing educ., 1996–present; adjunct graduate faculty, Clark U., MA, 1997–present; visiting asst. prof., TC, 1998–present.

Publications: Three Year Plan for Adult Basic Education, CT State Dept. of Educ., 1982; *Handbook on Competency Education*, with E. Strier, 1983; "Overcoming Barriers to Collaborative Learning: What Adult Students Can Teach Us," *Proceedings of What Works: Building Effective Collaborative Learning Experiences*, with B. Gonzalez, 1994.

Claire Canapary Macy
716 Martin Pond Road, Groton, MA 01450, (978) 448–6000, peteclaire@prodigy.net. b. Brooklyn, NY, Apr. 15, 1935. e. Massachusetts Gen. Hosp., 1953–56; TC, B.S., 1964–66; Springfield, M.H.S., 1976–78.

Employment: instr., Mt. Wachusetts CC, Gardner, MA; nurse practitioner (retired).

Anita R. Madea
3200 Capital Mall Drive SW, #C201, Olympia, WA 98502–8669, (360) 704–2915; dir. nursing, South Puget Sound CC, 2011 Mottman Road SW, Olympia, WA 98512. b. Plainfield, NJ, Dec. 19, 1950. e. Duke Sch. of Nursing, B.S.N., 1972; TC, M.A., 1980, Ed.M., 1981, Ed.D., 1985.

Employment: asst. prof., Intercollegiate Center for Nursing Educ., Washington State U. Coll. of Nursing, 1984–88; dir. nursing, South Puget Sound CC, 1999–present.

John J. Mahon
2371 Lower State Road, Doylestown, PA 18901, (215) 348–7659, jmahon@email.racc.pa.us; asst. to the pres. and dir. grants and

institutional planning, Reading Area CC, PO Box 1706, Reading, PA 19603. b. Washington, DC, Oct. 29, 1943. e. Penn State, B.A., 1965, M.Ed., 1966; TC, Ed.D., 1973.

Employment: Franklin Coll., dir., student activities and placement, 1966–67, dean of student affairs, 1967–69; Bucks County CC, PA, asst. to the pres., acting dir. of finance, and acting dir. of employee relations, 1972–85, interim dean of academic affairs and dean of student services, 1985–90; asst. to the pres. and dir. grants and institutional planning, Reading Area CC, PA, 1991–present.

Victor H. Margolis
788 Columbus Avenue, New York, NY 10025, (212) 666–8911, vmargol@worldnet.att.net. e. Temple Univ., B.A., 1959; TC, M.A and Ph.D., 1967.

Employment: counseling center/staff, Queensborough CC, NY, 1966–67; psychologist and prof., Nassau CC, 1967–97.

Publications: research articles, courses, government grants.

Maurice H. Margotta Jr.
2044 Glen Cove Drive, Seabrook, TX 77586, (281) 732–9991, mauredn@cs.com; corp. mgr., accounts receivable, Health Consultants, Inc., 9030 Monroe Road, Houston, TC 77061. b. Tarrytown, NY, Oct. 16, 1942. e. U. of Hartford, B.A., 1974, M.S., 1976; UConn, sixth-year diploma, 1981; Columbia, M.A., 1988, Ed.D., 1990.

Employment: adjunct prof., Tunxis Community Tech. Coll., 1976–85; prof., U. of Hartford, 1977–85; adjunct prof., Graduate Sch. of Credit and Financial Management, Dartmouth Coll., 1988–93; VP, Credit Research Foundation, 1985–94.

Publications: Credit Management, 1987; *Case Studies in Credit Management,* 1988; *Credit Management Home Study Course,* 1989; *Credit Management Review,* 1992; several articles for *Business Credit,* 1985–94.

Frances C. Marks
111 Highland Avenue, Middletown, NY 10940, (914) 343–4028. b. Minneapolis, MN, July 16, 1928. e. Lindenwood Coll., MO, 1947–48; Washington U. Sch. of Nursing, R.N., 1952, B.S., 1953; TC, M.S., 1966.

Employment: instr., Orange County Manpower Training Act (1 yr.); instr., CARE MEDICO, Afghanistan (1 mo.); instr., Orange County CC (13 yrs.); staff nurse, St. Louis Children's Hosp. (1 yr.); office nurse, private practice, NY (2 yrs.); staff nurse, Horton Memorial Hosp., (6 mos.); camp nurse, Camp Wishe, NY (10 yrs.); camp nurse, Vantage Point Tennis Camp, NY (1 yr.); consultant, CARE MEDICO, Indonesia (1 mo.).

Theodore Charles Markus
369 Marlborough Road, Cedarhurst, NY 11516, (516) 569–3452, tedcm@aol.com; prof. biology, Kingsborough CC, CUNY, 2001 Oriental Boulevard, Brooklyn, NY 11235. b. Brooklyn, NY, May 6, 1940. e. Brooklyn Coll., B.S., 1962; U. of Michigan, M.S., 1965; TC, M.Ed., 1987, Ed.D., 1988.
Employment: prof. of biology, Kingsborough CC, CUNY, 1966–present.
Publications: Learning Guide for Human Anatomy and Physiology (and instr. manual), 1987; "Remediation in American Higher Education: A New Phenomenon?" *Community Review*, vol. 8, with Arthur Zeitlin, 1992–93; "Should Remediation be Mandatory in the Community College?" *Community Review*, vol. 14, with Arthur Zeitlin, 1996; "AIDS Teaching Should Not be Limited to the Young," *USA Today*, with Richard Kaye, 1997.

Lois E. Marshall
31 Barnes Drive, Ridgefield Park, NJ 07600–1161, (201) 440–3199; dean of community services, 400 Paramus Road, Paramus, NJ 07652, (201) 447–1500, x212. b. New York, NY, May 11, 1932. e. Paterson State, NJ, B.A., 1963; Montclair State, NJ, M.A., 1967; TC, M.A., 1976, present-day doctoral candidate.
Employment: Ridgefield Park, NJ, teacher, English and speech, 1963–67, dir. adult education, 1966–67; dir. adult education, Plainfield, NJ, 1967–69; dean of community services and prof., 1969–present; appointed to the American Assoc. of Community and Junior Colleges, 1977.
Publications: "The Community College: A New Resource," *New Jersey Adult Educator*, 1970; "Action for Strengthening Family Well-Being," *Adult Leadership*, 1971; "Adult Learning Center: Bergen

Community College," *School Board Notes*, 1971; "Community College Profile: Introducing Bergen Community College," *The New Jersey Community College: A Professional Notebook*, 1971.

Patricia (Johnson) Maurer

84–19 51st Avenue, Elmhurst, NY 11373; assoc. prof., Queensborough CC, CUNY, 222–05 56th Avenue, Bayside, NY 11364. b. Cincinnati, OH, Mar. 31, 1930. e. U. of Cincinnati Coll. of Nursing, B.S.N., 1952; TC, M.A., 1957; New Sch. for Social Research, coursework in statistics and cybernetics, 1966–67; Hunter, CUNY, coursework in counseling and guidance, 1991–93.

Employment: asst. prof., U. of Cincinnati Coll. of Nursing, 1953–55; instr., coord., Lenox Hill Hosp. Sch. of Nursing, 1957–68; asst. and assoc. prof., Queensborough CC, CUNY, 1972–present.

Georgia McDuffie

524 Seven Oaks Road, Orange, NJ 07050, (973) 672–8699, ladyduffie@ aol.com; chair, nursing dept., Medgar Evers Coll., 1150 Carroll Street, Brooklyn, NY 11225. b. Perry, GA. e. Essex County Coll., NJ, A.A.S., 1972; Long Island U., B.S.N., 1973; Columbia, M.A., 1975; Seton Hall, M.A., 1977; Walden U., MN, Ph.D., 1987.

Employment: instr., nursing, Essex County Coll., 1973–75; coord. and instr., Seton Hall U., 1975–77; dir. of educ., NJ State Nurses Assoc., 1977–79; dept. chair, Bucks County CC, 1979–85; division chair, health science dept., Roxbury CC, MA, 1985–86; assoc. dean and division chair, allied health and nursing programs, Mass Bay CC, 1986–88; admin. supervisor, East Orange Gen. Hosp., NJ, 1988–90; dir. of nursing, Essex Valley Visiting Nurse Assoc., NJ, 1992–99; chair, dept. of nursing, Medgar Evers Coll., NY, 2001–present.

Earl J. McGrath

b. Buffalo, NY, Nov. 16, 1902. e. U. of Buffalo, B.A., 1928, M.A., 1930; U. of Chicago, Ph.D., 1936. d. Tucson, AZ, Jan. 14, 1993.

Employment: faculty and admin., U. of Buffalo, fellow, U. of Chicago, educ. consultant, 1928–42; Lt. Commander, educ. services, U.S. Navy, 1942–44; dean, Coll. of Liberal Arts, U. of Iowa, 1945–48; prof., U. of Chicago, 1948–49; U.S. Commissioner of Educ., 1949–53;

admin. and prof., U. of Kansas, Columbia U., Temple U., and U. of Arizona, 1953–93.

M. Margaret McIntosh
1401 Queen Street, Cornwall, Ontario, Canada K6J 1R3, (613) 933–3691. b. Cornwall, Ontario, Canada, Feb. 1, 1920. e. St. Joseph's Sch. of Nursing, Cornwall, Ontario, Canada; McGill Sch. for Graduate Nurses; TC, B.Sc.Ed.
Employment: sr. staff nurse, City of Montreal Health Dept., 1944–55; asst. dir. of nursing, City of Ottawa Health Dept., 1955–58; supervisor and admin., nursing services, Carleton County Health Unit, Ottawa, 1958–66; lecturer, Queen's U. Sch. of Nursing, Ontario, 1966–68; dir. nursing, Eastern Ontario Health Unit, 1969–85.

Richard J. Meagher
85 Vincent Place, Lynbrook, NY 11563, (516) 599–9122, rjumeagher@aol.com; dean emeritus for continuing educ., Fashion Institute of Technology, 7th Avenue at 27th Street, New York, NY 10001. b. Lynbrook, NY, Oct. 8, 1938. e. Long Island U., B.A., 1960, M.A., 1962; TC, Ed.D., 1983.
Employment: graduate asst., Long Island U., 1960–62; lecturer, Baruch Coll., 1962–64; Fashion Institute of Technology, lecturer, 1963–65, asst. dir., special studies and evening programs, 1965–70, asst. dean, special studies and evening programs, 1970–72, assoc. dean for continuing educ., 1972–77, dean of continuing educ., 1977–94, consultant in academic affairs, 1988–99.
Publications: "Making the Case for the Establishment of Weekend Colleges at SUNY Community Colleges," *Insight*, 1979; "January Minisemesters: A Specialized Tool for SUNY Community Colleges," *Insight*, 1980; "The Weekend College: Prescription for the Eighties?" *Continuing Higher Education*, 1981; "Citizens' Advisory Committees: A Tool in Every District's Toolbox," *Journal of the New York State School Boards Association*, 1990.

Herbert Merrill, II
35 Deepwood Court, Amherst, NY 14228, (716) 564–0509, merrill@ ecc.edu; pres., faculty council of community colleges, Erie CC, SUNY

Plaza, S300, Albany, NY 12246. b. Mar. 9, 1942. e. SUNY, B.A., 1971, M.Ed., 1973, M.S., 1983; TC, Ed.D., 1996.

Employment: SUNY Buffalo, 1971–77; Buffalo State Coll., 1977–79; Erie CC, prof. and dir., college counseling center and admissions, 1979–99, faculty council of community colleges, 1999–present.

Andrew L. Meyer
700 Washington Place, Unit 4C, Baltimore, MD 21201, (410) 385–2407, almeyer@mail.aacc.cc.md.us; VP for Learning, Anne Arundel CC, 101 College Parkway, Arnold, MD 21012. b. Wisconsin, Sept. 11, 1955. e. U. of Wisconsin, Milwaukee, B.S., 1978; U. of Maryland, M.Ed., 1982; TC, M.A., 1989, Ed.D., 1989; Institute for the Management of Lifelong Educ., Harvard, 1995.

Employment: dir., community services and special programs, and dir., ESL and international educ., CC of Baltimore, 1980–85; dir., noncredit program, Towson State U., 1985–86; asst. dean, continuing educ. and community services, CC of Baltimore; dir., continuing educ. and community services, Carroll CC, 1987–89; Anne Arundel CC, asst. dean, continuing educ., 1989–92, dean, continuing educ. and extended learning programs, 1992–96, VP, continuing educ. and workforce development, 1996–2000; VP for Learning, 2000–present; consultant, Frederick CC, 1994 and 1997, and Community Colleges of Baltimore County, 1998; commissioner, American Assoc. of Community Colleges' Commission on Economic and Workforce Development, 1997–99.

Publications: co-author, "Community Colleges and Workforce Training: Past Performance and Future Directions," *The Maryland Association for Higher Education Journal*, 1995; contributor, *Developing the World's Best Workforce: An Agenda for America's Community Colleges*, 1997.

Claire Ricci Meyer
PO Box 766, Sag Harbor, NY 11963–0019, (631) 725–3284. b. Easton, PA, Apr. 5, 1925. e. Morovian Coll., PA, B.S., 1966; Lehigh U., PA, M.A.; TC, M.A., 1980, M.Ed., 1981.

Employment: prof. mental illness and mental health and curriculum chair, Northampton CC (20 yrs.).

Publications: several book reviews for the *American Journal of Nursing*.

Sergei Mikhelson
1944 Bay Ridge Parkway, #6, Brooklyn, NY 11204, (718) 259–8444, ssm21@columbia.edu; adjunct prof., math dept., Borough of Manhattan CC, 199 Chambers Street, New York, NY 10007. b. St. Petersburg, Russia, May 17, 1970. e. Russian State Pedagogical U., bachelor's degree, 1992, master's degree, 1993; TC, M.A., 1994, present-day Ph.D. candidate; The Johns Hopkins U., Institute for Policy Studies, 1993.

Employment: math tutor, independent school Razvitie, St. Petersburg, Russia, 1987–91; board member, coed., Educational Limited Co., St. Petersburg, Russia, 1989–present; educ. advisor, Parents' Charitable Assoc., 1991–93; teacher, mathematics and logic, experimental secondary school no. 56, St. Petersburg, Russia, 1991–98; intern, Parents Anonymous of Maryland, Inc., 1993; tutor, Columbia U. Tutoring Service, 1993–94; research consultant, Connected Mathematics Project, Queens Coll., NY, 1994; laboratory head, Center for Alternative Education Development of the City Board of Educ., St. Petersburg, Russia, 1994–98; prof. logic and argumentation theory, The Nevsky Institute for Russian Studies, St. Petersburg, Russia, 1997–98; math tutor, Intellect Consulting Center, NY, 1998–present; adjunct lecturer, Borough of Manhattan CC, 1998–present; adjunct instr., NYU, 1999–present.

Publications: "Can the Present Studying Activity Be Considered Group Establishing?" *Towards New School*, Leningrad, 1989; "School of Mathematical Culture," *Towards New School*, Leningrad, 1991; "Mathematics Education in Russian," *Encyclopedia of Mathematics Education*, 2001.

Belinda S. Miles
12000 Fairhill Road, #213, Cleveland, OH 44120, (216) 707–0271, belinda.miles@tri-c.cc.oh.us; interim asst. dean, Cuyahoga CC, 2900 Community College Avenue, Cleveland, OH 44115, (216) 987–4537. b. Queens, NY, July 3, 1961. e. York Coll., CUNY, B.A., 1983; TC, M.A., 1988, Ed.D., 2000.

Employment: ITT Educ. Services, NY, admissions rep., 1983–85, dir. of job placement, 1985–86; instr., LaGuardia CC, CUNY, 1986–90; dir. of field services, NY State Governor's Sch. and Business Alliance, 1990–93; Nassau CC, SUNY, program dir., Educ. for Gainful Employment and Adult Individualized Multi-Services, 1993–95, instr., 1995; TC, admin. assoc., National Center for Restructuring, Educ., Schools, and Teaching, 1995–96, teaching asst., 1996; project dir., Queens School-to-Work Opportunities, LaGuardia CC, CUNY, 1996–97; mgr., staff and special project admin., Columbia Sch. of Law, 1997–99; Cuyahoga CC, OH, interim asst. dean, 2000, special projects consultant, 2000, interim asst. dean, 2001–present; instr., U. of Akron, 2000.

Publications: Composition and Critical Thinking Through Cooperative Education, 1990; "Motivational and Success Factors for Job Opportunities and Basic Skills (JOBS) Program Clients," presented to the Community College General Educ. Assoc., 1995.

Adele Miller
3201 Taft Street, Hollywood, FL 33021. b. New York, NY, Mar. 22, 1918. e. NY Hosp., R.N., 1941; U. of Miami, B.S.; TC, M.A., 1958.

Employment: instr. and dir. of nursing program, Broward CC (7 yrs.).

Dorothy W. Miller
342 Harlan Square, Bel Air, MD 21014, (410) 838–0170, dotti@ starpower.net; English prof., Harford CC, 401 Thomas Run Road, Bel Air, MD 21015. b. Fort Pierce, FL, Apr. 13, 1944. e. Bloomsburg U., B.S., 1966, M.Ed., 1969; Johns Hopkins U., M.L.A., 1978; TC, Ed.D., 1991.

Estelle L. Miller
494 East 18th Street, Brooklyn, NY 11226, (718) 284–1566; Kingsborough CC, CUNY, (718) 368–5157, emiller@kbcc.cuny.edu. e. Brooklyn Coll., CUNY, B.A., 1971; Catholic U. Sch. of Social Service, M.S.W., 1974; 5th Avenue Center for Counseling and Psychotherapy, completed 3 yrs. of training, 1975–78; TC, Ed.D., 1997.

Employment: psychotherapist, 5th Avenue Center and Guidance Center of Flatbush, NY, 1975–82; Kingsborough CC, CUNY, asst. prof., dept. of student development, 1983–present, coord. returning adults program, 1990–98, adjunct instr., 1994–97, coord. student development for College Now program, 1998–present, dir. women's center, 1999–present.

Publications: book review, "'Ivory Power: Sexual Harassment on Campus,' by Dr. Michele Paludi," *American Assoc. of Women in Community and Junior Colleges Quarterly,* 1991; "University Services: New Vistas for College Student Personnel," *College Personnel Assoc. Journal,* 1998; "Meeting the Challenge: A Qualitative Study of Female Reentry Students at a Community College," *Michigan Community College Journal,* 2000.

Joan M. Millett
198 Kings Highway, West Springfield, MA 01089–2529, (413) 739–8020. b. Bristol, CT, Feb. 13, 1930. e. St. Joseph Coll., CT, B.S., 1951; TC, M.A., 1954; UMass Sch. of Educ., C.A.G.S. in educ., 1985.

Employment: instr. and supervisor, obstetrics, Norwalk Hosp., 1952–53; instr., Boston Lying-In Hosp., 1954–56; instr., St. Joseph Coll., CT, 1956–58; instr., UMass, 1958–59 and 1967–70; prof. nursing, Springfield Technical CC, 1970–94.

Mildred L. Montag
111 Cherry Valley Avenue, #310, Garden City, NY 11530, (516) 746–7268; prof. emeritus, nursing educ., TC. b. Struble, IA, Aug. 10, 1908. e. Hamline U., MN, A.B., 1930; U. of Minnesota, B.S., 1933; TC, M.A., 1938, Ed.D., 1950; honorary degrees received include U. of Bridgeport, LL.D., 1967, Adelphi U., L.H.D., 1968, SUNY, LL.D., 1981, U. of Eastern Kentucky, D.Sc., 1981, and American Academy of Nursing, Honorary Fellow, 1985.

Employment: nursing instructor, Lincoln Gen. Hosp. Sch. of Nursing, NE, 1933–35, U. of Minnesota Sch. of Nursing, 1935–37, St. Luke's Hosp. Sch. of Nursing, NY, 1938–41; staff nurse, Henry Street Visiting Nurse Service, NY, 1941; asst. dir., nurse testing division, Psychological Corp., NY, 1942; staff member, U.S. Public Health Service, Washington, DC, 1942; founder and dir., Adelphi

Coll. Sch. of Nursing, NY, 1942–48; TC, instructor, nursing educ., 1948–50, prof., nursing educ., 1950–72; dir., Cooperative Research Project in Junior and Community College Educ. for Nursing, 1952–57; visiting prof., U. of Colorado Sch. of Nursing, summer sessions, 1966–68; affiliated with numerous other colleges and organizations through workshops and consultations.

Publications: Pharmacology and Therapeutics, with Harold N. Wright; *Fundamentals in Nursing Care*, with Ruth P. Swenson; *Education of Nurse Technicians*; *Community College Education for Nursing*; *Evaluation of Graduates of Associate Degree Nursing Programs*; *Nursing Concepts and Nursing Care*, with Alice Rines; *Handbook of Fundamental Nursing Techniques*, with Alice Rines; contributed to *Comprehensive Review of Nursing*, Mosby, and *Technical Nursing*, Sandra Rasmussen; numerous articles in *Teachers College Record*, *Nursing Outlook*, and *American Journal of Nursing*.

Toni Thomas Moumouris
22 Oak Ridge Drive, Brooklyn, CT 06234, qv_moumouris@ commnet.edu; enrollment and transition counselor, Quinebaug Valley CC, 742 Upper Maple Street, Danielson, CT 06239. b. Putnam, CT, Apr. 23, 1955. e. Central CT State U., B.S., 1977, M.S., 1979; TC, Ed.D., 1997.

Employment: assoc. dir. of admissions, Central CT State U., 1978–88; Tunxis Community-Technical Coll., dir. of placement and transfer, 1998–91, acting dir. of admissions, 1990–91, acting dir. of records and placement, 1992, counselor and student development specialist, 1994–97, dir. of student development center, 1997–99; Quinebaug Valley CC, enrollment and transition counselor, 1999–present.

Publications: dissertation, *Successful Community College Transfer Students: Academic Performance, Enrollment Behavior, and Baccalaureate Degree Attainment*.

Mary Mowrey-Raddock
125 Turner Road, Stamford, CT 06905, (203) 461–9626, nk_raddock@commnet.edu; prof., Norwalk CC, 188 Richards Avenue, Norwalk, CT 06854. b. Corry, PA, May 16, 1947. e. William Smith Coll., B.A., 1965–69; TC, M.A., 1975; Ed.D., 1979.

Employment: financial aid and residential life, Marymount Manhattan Coll., 1975–78; asst. VP of student affairs, Fordham U., 1978–86; adjunct assoc. prof., TC, 1986–91; Norwalk CC, dean of students, 1991–98, prof., 1998–present.

Joan C. Mullaney
6 Morningside Park, Pittsford, NY 14534, (716) 334–0421, jmullaney@monroecc.edu; prof., human services, Monroe CC, Damon Center, 228 East Main Street, Rochester, NY 14604. b. Jamestown, NY, Mar. 22, 1943.
Employment: began a thirty-year teaching career at Monroe CC in 1971 as faculty, general studies; program dir., Tuesday Thursday Coll. (for returning women students), 1979–91; prof., human services, 1991–present.

Frances R. Nichols
Box 33, Molina, CO 81646, (970) 268–5491. b. Jireh, WY, Oct. 10, 1920. e. Wyoming U., 1939; Weber State Coll., 1952; TC, M.A., 1958; U. of Utah, 1959.
Employment: elementary teacher (6 yrs.); instr., nursing educ. (38 yrs.).

Verona "Ronnie" Blackmore Oard
2520 Keystone Court North, St. Petersburg, FL 33710, (727) 381–3227, oards@aol.com; self-employed consultant. b. Englewood, NJ, Sept. 2, 1943. e. Washington U., B.A., 1965 (transferred from Trenton State Coll.); TC, M.A., 1970.
Employment: asst. to VP, sales and marketing, Modern Talking Picture Service, 1966–69; dir. financial aid, Marymount Coll., 1969–72; dir. financial aid, SUNY Farmingdale, 1972–75; asst. prof., counseling and financial aid, Suffolk County CC, 1975–79; financial aid counselor, St. Petersburg Jr. Coll., 1979–87; VP, regional sales exec., National Sales Training Exec. Educ. Finance Center and Chase Manhattan Bank, 1987–95; VP, national accounts, Chase Manhattan Bank and Sallie Mae; VP, regional business, American Express Educ. Loans, 1997–99; consultant, Hillsborough CC, 1999–present.
Publications: Financial Aid Wall Charts, 1976.

Pearline Okumakpeyi
1360 East 40th Street, Brooklyn, NY 11234, (718) 951–3822,
okumakpeyi@aol.com; assoc. prof., NYC Technical Coll., 300 Jay
Street, Brooklyn, NY 11201. b. July 11, 1952. e. Hunter Coll.,
CUNY, 1974; TC, M.A., 1979, M.Ed., 1993.
   Employment: National Technical Teachers Coll., Lagos Nigeria,
West Africa, 1980–83; clinical performance examiner, Regents Coll.
External Degree Nursing Program, 1987–97; adjunct prof., Borough of
Manhattan CC, 1989–99; assoc. prof., nursing, NYC Technical Coll.,
1985–present.

Cheryl Opacinch
2625 Woodley Place NW, Washington, DC 20008, (202) 232–4338,
cheryl.opacinch@DTRA.mil; Sr. Foreign Affairs Advisor, Dept. of
Defense, U.S. Government, DoD/DTRA/ST, Suite 300, 400 Army
Navy Drive, Arlington, VA 22202. b. Dunkirk, NY, Apr. 17, 1944. e.
SUNY Buffalo, B.S., 1966; TC, M.A., 1967, Ed.D., 1971.
   Employment: TC, admin. asst., Horace Mann Lincoln Institute,
1967–68, asst. to the department chair, higher and adult educ.,
1968–70; Catonsville CC, 1970–75; post-doctoral government fellow,
American Council on Educ., 1975–76; consultant to the U.S. govern-
ment, Dept. of Educ., 1977–78.
   Publications: numerous writings about institutional research in com-
munity colleges.

Florence Anne Pallein
3365 Genoa Way, #140, Oceanside, CA 92056, (760) 439–6469.
b. Manchester, CT, Sept. 5, 1926. e. Hartford Hosp. Sch. of Nursing,
R.N., 1947; Boston U. Sch. of Nursing, B.S., 1951; TC, M.A., 1953;
Nova U., FL, Ed.D., 1979.
   Employment: UConn Sch. of Nursing, 1953–55; UC Westwood,
1955–58; clinical coord., Queen of Angels Hosp., CA, 1961–62;
Golden West CC, CA, 1970–83.
   Publications: dissertation, *Evaluation of Modular Instruction in
Terms of Student Achievement and Instr./Student Attitudes in the
Golden West Community College Nursing Program,* 1979.

Constance Mills Palmer

20 Sunset Road, New London, CT 06320, (860) 443–2262. b. New London, CT, Jan. 24, 1925. e. Mass Gen. Hosp. Sch. of Nursing, 1948; Mitchell Coll., A.S., 1958; U. of Bridgeport, B.S., 1961; TC, M.A., 1963.

Employment: Joseph Lawrence Sch. of Nursing; U. of Rhode Island, 1963–73; Mohegan CC, 1973–86.

Faye Pappalardo

63 Hook Road, Westminster, MD 21157, (410) 871–2571, fpappalardo@carroll.cc.md.us; pres., Carroll CC, 1601 Washington Road, Westminster, MD 21157. b. Philadelphia, PA, Sept. 25, 1931. e. Mt. St. Mary's U., MD, B.S., 1960; L'Institut Catholique de Paris, diploma, French studies, 1970; Catholic U. of America, master equivalency, 1971; Johns Hopkins U., M.S., 1978; Columbia, M.A., 1991, Ed.D., 1992.

Employment: teacher, Towson Catholic, MD, and others, 1966–68; junior high school instr., St. Lawrence, MD, 1968–70; instr., guidance counselor, and foreign language dept. chair, Catholic Girls' HS, MD, 1970–72; dean, Bay Coll. of Maryland, 1972–76; consultant, Science Research Assoc., NY, 1972–74; long range planning asst., National Center for College and University Long Range Planning, MD, 1977–78; CC of Baltimore, dir. of student life, 1978–86, dean of student affairs, 1986–88; Carroll CC, MD, dir. of student affairs, 1988–91, asst. to the exec. dean and dir. of student affairs, 1991–92, exec. VP, 1992–96, exec. VP of teaching, learning, and institutional planning, 1996–98, assoc. pres., 1998–99, pres., 1999–present.

Publications: dissertation, *Adult Educators' Responses to Selected Issues of Practice*, 1992.

Marie E. (Leis) Pearce

639 Pontiac Road, Oxford, MI 48371–4850, (248) 628–3589, suttonpl@tir.com. b. Saranac Lake, NY, May 18, 1913. e. Barnard, B.A., 1935; Yale Sch. of Nursing, M.N., 1938; TC, M.A., 1943.

Employment: head, nursing dept., Oakland CC, MI (retired).

Dolores Perin
201 W. 89th St., Apt 2H, New York, NY 10024, (212) 678–3943, dp111@columbia.edu.
Employment: Associate Professor of Psychology and Education at Teachers College, Columbia University.
Publications: several papers on topics such as academic-occupational integration in community colleges, the literacy skills of community-college developmental education students, as well as a faculty development guide for integrated instruction in community colleges.

Christopher G. Potter
1308 Laurel Point Circle, Harrisburg, PA 17110, (717) 233–0556; sr. prof. of psychology and counseling, Harrisburg Area CC, 1 HACC Drive, Harrisburg, PA 17104. b. New York, NY, Sept. 2, 1944. e. Hamilton Coll., B.A., 1966; Queens Coll., graduate psych., 1968; TC, M.A., 1972.
Employment: teacher, grade school, NY, 1968–71; Harrisburg Area CC, prof. and counselor, 1972–present, ombudsperson, 1989–99; recipient of NISON award for teaching excellence in community colleges, 1988 and 2000.
Publications: "The Gestalt of Student Lives and the Educational Experience," *Humanizing Student Services*, Clyde E. Blocker, ed., 1974.

Pascale M. Pritsios
220 North Saint Asaph Street, #15, Alexandria, VA 22314, (202) 663–5640, pascale_pritsios@yahoo.com; assoc. dir. of alumni relations and the annual fund, The Paul H. Nitze Sch. of Advanced Studies, Johns Hopkins U., 1740 Massachusetts Avenue NW, Washington, DC, 20036. b. York, PA, June 8, 1973. e. Bucknell, B.A., 1995; TC, M.A., 2000.
Employment: Jerome Chazen Institute for International Business, alumni relations officer, 1998–99, assoc. dir., 1999–2001; dir. alumni relations and annual fund, Paul H. Nitze Sch. of Advanced Studies, Johns Hopkins U., 2001–present.

Kathleen Jester Prokop
36 Rockwood Road, Florham Park, NJ 07932, (973) 301–2073, kprokop@ccm.edu; assoc. prof. nursing, County Coll. of Morris, 214

Center Grove Road, Randolph, NJ 07869. b. Wilmington, DE, Dec. 24, 1965. e. Georgetown, B.S.N., 1987; TC, M.A., Ed.D., 1988–92. *Employment:* nursing instr., County Coll. of Morris, 1992–present.

Susanne Ptak
121 Highland Avenue, Middletown, NY 10940, (845) 343–4666; prof. emerita, Orange County CC, South Street, Middletown, NY 10940. b. Newburgh, NY, Apr. 27, 1935. e. St. Luke's Hosp. Sch. of Nursing, 1954–57; TC, B.S., 1963, M.A., 1968.
Employment: St. Luke's Hosp., staff nurse, 1957–58, clinical instr., 1958–64; Orange County CC, clinical instr., 1964–68, asst. and assoc. prof., nursing, 1968–99, prof. emerita and p/t clinical, 1999–present.

Martin S. Quigley
8 Pheasant Run, Larchmont, NY 10538, (914) 654–0533, greatgaels @aol.com; chr., Quigley Publishing Co., Inc., 9 Railroad Way, Larchmont, NY 10538. b. Chicago, IL, Nov. 24, 1917. e. Loyola Sch., NY, 1931–35; Georgetown, B.A., 1935–39; TC, M.A., 1973, Ed.D., 1975.
Employment: consulting partnership in higher educ. with Ira Weinberg, 1975–80; adjunct prof., Baruch Coll., Seton Hall U., and TC, 1977–90; short-term English instr. in Poland and Italy.
Publications: Great Gaels, 1944; *Roman Notes,* 1946; *Magic Shadows: The Story of the Origin of Motion Pictures,* 1948; ed., *New Screen Techniques,* 1953; co-author, *Catholic Action in Practice,* 1963; co-author, *Films in America,* 1970; dissertation, *Government Relations of Five Universities in Washington, D.C.,* 1975; *Peace Without Hiroshima: Secret Action at the Vatican in the Spring of 1945,* 1991, Japanese edition, 1992; *A U.S. Spy in Ireland,* 1999; numerous articles on film and education.

Lois H. Rafenski
30 Lincoln Road, Bethpage, NY 11714, (516) 938–7817, lhrafenski@ aol.com; prof., SUNY Coll. of Technology, Melville Road, Farmingdale, NY 11735. b. Bethpage, NY, Aug. 25, 1937. e. SUNY Farmingdale, A.A.S., R.N., 1962–64; Adelphi U., B.S., 1968; TC, Ed.M., 1971, Ed.D., 1982.

Employment: assoc. degree nursing dept., SUNY Coll. of Technology, 1971–present.

Judith F. Raulf
5 Cramer Drive, Chester, NJ 07930, (973) 584–4552, jraulf@ccm.edu; dean of liberal arts, County Coll. of Morris, 214 Center Grove Road, Randolph, NJ 07869, (973) 328–5400. b. Trenton, NJ, July 29, 1940. e. Rider U., NJ, A.A., 1967, B.S.Ed., 1969, M.A., 1973; Rutgers U., Ed.S., 1984; TC, Ed.D., 1992.
Employment: Rider U., NJ, adjunct instr. and dir. of student services, Sch. of Continuing Studies, 1969–73; Morris County Coll., NJ, adjunct lecturer, 1973–95, counselor and evaluator, 1973–75, asst. dean of academic affairs, 1975–88, dean of curriculum and instruction, 1988–96, dean of liberal arts, 1996–present.
Publications: with M. C. Ayres, "The Challenge of Curriculum Development: From Idea to Reality," in *Developing Occupational Programs—New Directions for Community Colleges*, C. R. Doty, ed., 1987; dissertation, *An Institutional Evaluation of Perceptions and Expectations of Prior Learning Assessment Programs*, 1992; "Headquarters Plaza—From Concept to Reality," *Update*, 1995.

Claire J. Reilly
9 Merry Hill Road, Poughkeepsie, NY 12603–3213, (845) 462–2167. b. New York, NY, Mar. 2, 1925. e. Mt. Sinai Hosp. Sch. of Nursing, 1943–45; Dutchess CC, A.A.S., 1960–62; TC, B.S., 1964, M.A., 1966; SUNY New Paltz and Albany, post-grad. study, 1968–70; certified guidance counselor.
Employment: Dutchess CC, nursing instr., 1964–66, asst. prof., maternal and child health and major health problems, 1966–70; guidance counselor, Newburgh City Schools.

Mary Eleanor Reiter
610 East 1st Street, #1–4, Spring Valley, IL 61362–1580. b. Homestead, PA, July 11, 1912. e. LaSalle-Peru-Oglesby Jr. Coll., A.A., 1929–31; Northwestern, B.S., 1931–33; Johns Hopkins Hosp., R.N., 1937; NYU, nursing educ. courses, 1943–47; TC, M.A., 1947–48; U of Minnesota, M.Ph., 1951–53.

Employment: student nurse orientation, emergency pavilion, New York Hosp., 1943; faculty, Long Island Coll. Hosp. Sch. of Nursing, 1943–47; researcher, NY Academy of Medicine, 1948–49; nursing consultant, Georgia Dept. of Maternal and Child Health, 1949–51; staff, VA Hosp., IL, 1953–55; psych. instr. and supervisor, Chicago Wesley Hosp., 1955–57; nursing educ. faculty, NYU, 1957–58; faculty, Graduate Sch. of Nursing, NY Medical Coll., 1962–64; Rockford Singer Center, Illinois Dept. of Mental Health, 1965–66; faculty and founder of nursing program, Illinois Valley CC, 1967–70; faculty, Columbus Jr. Coll., GA, 1970–72.

Publications: "Educating Adolescents to Become Nurses," *American Journal of Nursing*; "Back Then," *Vigilando*, 1999.

Ileana Rodriguez

6 Seasongood Road, Forest Hills, NY 11375, (718) 261–5944, irg@nyts.edu; acting pres., New York Theological Seminary, 5 West 29th Street, New York, NY 10001, (212) 532–4012. b. San Juan, Puerto Rico, Nov. 12, 1949. e. Coll. of the Sacred Heart, PR, B.A., 1968; U. of Puerto Rico, M.P.A., 1974; TC, M.Ed., 1988, Ed.D.; Harvard, post-grad., 1988.

Employment: U.S. Dept. of Housing and Urban Devlopment, urban intern, 1968–69, management officer, 1969–74; adjunct prof., Central U. and Inter-American U., PR, 1972–74; adjunct prof., City Coll., Lehman Coll., and Kingsborough CC, 1974–76; asst. and deputy dir. of personnel, Lincoln Medical and Health Center, NY, 1976–79; personnel dir., Greenpoint Hosp., NY, 1979–81; adjunct prof., St. Joseph's Coll., NY, 1980–85; VP human resources, Bronx-Lebanon Hosp. Center, 1981–82; assoc. exec. dir., human resources, Woodhull Medical and Mental Health Center, NY, 1982–85; VP admin., NY City Technical Coll., 1985–90; deputy to the pres. and dean of finance and admin., Hostos CC, CUNY, 1990–92; adjunct prof., NY City Technical Coll., 1992–99; adjunct prof., Central Michigan U., 1992–present; NY Theogical Seminary, COO and VP, 1993–2000, prof. of church and community, 1993–present, CEO and acting pres., 2000–present.

Maura Cowherd Rose

1 Park Court, Middletown, NY 10940, (845) 342–2459, willrose1@ hotmail.com; asst. nursing prof., Orange County CC, 15 South Street,

Middletown, NY 10940. b. Havana, Cuba, Aug. 18, 1954. e. Orange County CC, A.S., 1974; SUNY, B.S.N., 1977; TC, M.A., 1995.

Employment: instr., L.P.N. prog., Philadelphia sch. district, 1979–82; nursing instr., Orange County CC, 1983–present.

Publications: "One Child's Reaction to Acute Pain," *Nursing Clinics of North America*, 1977.

Mordecai Rubin

283 Odell Avenue, Yonkers, NY 10703, (914) 966–0977, mrubin@aol.com. b. June 20, 1930, Brooklyn, NY. e. Rutgers, A.B., 1955; National U. of Mexico, A.M., 1957; U. of Maryland, Ph.D., 1961.

Employment: teaching positions with the following: Academia Garza, Mexico, 1954–56; Gannon U., PA, 1956–59; Cathedral HS, PA, 1958–59; Washington Coll., MD, 1959–62; Clark U., MA, 1962–65; New York CC, Brooklyn, 1966–70; prof. of Spanish and head, foreign language graduate studies and teacher training, TC, 1965–present; Fort Lee HS, NJ, 1988–89.

Publications: Una Poetica Moderna, 1966; "A Modern Methodology for Teaching Chinese," *Journal of the American Association of Teachers of Chinese*, 1968; "La ensenanza de la poesia," *Cuadernos Literarios*, 1996; "La Generacion de 98: alma espanola y concepto de la vida," *Cuadernos*, 1999; A *Sotto Voce*, 2001; numerous collections of original poetry and translations.

Vincent T. Rudan

157 East 72nd Street, #8GH, (212) 744–2512, prof157@aol.com; asst. prof., Lehman Coll., 250 Bedford Park Boulevard West, Bronx, NY 10468–1589. b. New York, NY, June 19, 1955. e. SUNY Stony Brook, B.S.N., 1977; NYU, M.A., 1979; TC, Ed.D., 1998.

Employment: nursing instr., Rutgers U., 1980–83; dir. of patient care services, Manhattan Eye and Ear Hosp., 1983–98; asst. nursing prof., Lehman Coll., 1998–present; adjunct asst. prof., TC, 1998–present.

Publications: with K. Frederickson, "Where Will Tomorrow's Nurse Managers Come From?" *Journal of Nursing Administration* 30 (2000); "Is it Time to Eliminate Education Departments? Take the

Lead from the Corporate World," *Journal of Nursing Administration* 31 (2001).

Elizabeth St. John-Speakman
148 East Partridge Lane, Cherry Hill, NJ 08003, (856) 751–8237, espeakman@ccp.cc.pa.us; assoc. prof., nursing, CC of Philadelphia, 1700 Spring Garden Street, Philadelphia, PA 19130. b. Brooklyn, NY, Oct. 3, 1958. e. Wagner Coll., B.S.N., 1980; TC, M.Ed., 1985, Ed.D., 2000.
   Employment: CC of Philadelphia, asst. prof., 1989–98, assoc. prof., 1998–present.
   Publications: "Associate Degree Nursing Education Today: Myths and Realities," *Imprint*, with E. Tagliareni and A. Mengel, 1998; "Fluid and Electrolyte, Acid-Base Balance," *Basic Nursing*, Potter and Perry, eds., 1999; "Fluid and Electrolyte, Acid-Base Balance," *Fundamental of Nursing*, Potter and Perry, eds., 2000.

Helen Norman Saputo
46–43 Douglaston Parkway, Douglaston, NY 11362–1056, (718) 229–1380, hns5@msn.com; prof., Queensborough CC, CUNY, 222–05 56th Avenue, Bayside, NY 11364–1497. b. Far Rockaway, NY. e. Hunter Coll., NY, B.A., 1955, M.S., 1983; Columbia, M.A., 1983, completed all coursework toward Ed.D.
   Employment: secretary, CIT Financial, 1948–55; teacher, Interboro Institute of Business, Inc., 1955–59; teacher, Small Business Sch., 1959–66; teacher, Bayside high sch. community center, 1965–66; teacher, Western Electric Co., 1966; teacher, American Management Assoc., 1966–68; lecturer, Hunter Coll., 1966–68; lecturer, LaGuardia CC, 1971–72; Queensborough CC, CUNY, adjunct lecturer, 1967, instr., 1968–70, asst. prof., 1971–74, assoc. prof., 1975–79, prof., 1980–present.
   Publications: co-author, "How to Provide Human Relations Instruction on Community College Technology Programs," *American Vocational Journal*, 1972; co-author, *Medical Secretary's Standard Reference Handbook*, 1980; co-author, *Secretary's New Guide to Dealing with People*, 1986.

Sylvia Schudy
104 Seacord Road, New Rochelle, NY 10804, (914) 632–5330. b. New York, NY, May 30, 1924. e. Westchester Sch. of Nursing, R.N.; TC, B.S., 1952, M.A., 1962, post-masters credit.

Employment: dir. nursing educ. and allied health programs, Norwalk CC, 1967–96; developed the first assoc. degree nursing program in a CT public community college; previous experience includes assoc. dir. of nursing educ., instr., medical-surgical nursing and operating room supervisor.

Publications: ed. and contributor, *Comprehensive Psychiatric Nursing.*

Eugene Schumacher
631 Walnut Street, Weed, CA 96094, (530) 938–4522, eschutv@ inreach.com. b. Tracy, MN, Dec. 26, 1925. e. Minot State Teacher's Coll., NROTC, 1944; Westminster Coll., B.A., 1949; U. of Minnesota, summer session, 1950; TC, M.A., 1954; UCLA, Ed.D., 1971.

Employment: U.S. Navy, 1943–46; lifeguard, 1953; Ford Foundation fellowship, Columbia U., 1953–54; draftsman and cartographer, Elko County Assessor's Office, 1955; Elko County HS, math teacher, NV, 1949–53, math teacher and counselor, 1954–55, vice principal and counselor, 1955–56; superintendent of schools, Eureka County Sch. District, 1956–58; Antelope Valley Coll., CA, asst. dean of students, 1958–61, dean of student personnel services, 1961–67, dean of instruction, 1967–70; pres. and superintendent, Siskiyou Joint CC District, CA, 1970–92.

Rita Serotkin
10 Baldwin Street, Pennington, NJ 08534, (609) 737–0478, ritas29@aol.com; asst. dir., Center for Educ., Widener U., 1 University Place, Chester, PA 19013. b. Newark, NJ, Feb. 9, 1947. e. Douglass Coll., B.A., 1964–68; Harvard, coursework in social relations, 1966; TC, M.A., 1968–70; Mercer County CC, misc. coursework, 1980–2000; Widener U., currently enrolled in Ed.D. program.

Employment: Coll. of NJ, coord. of student services and instr. of psychology, 1971–74, academic advisor, 1979–82; staff assoc., test ed., Educational Testing Service, 1982–87; professional staff, coord. of academic testing services, academic affairs admin., dir. of noncredit records, registration, and programs, Mercer County CC, 1987–2000; asst. dir. and instr., Center for Educ., Widener U., 2000–present.

Publications: "College for the Non-College Age," *Rutgers Alumni Magazine*, 1974; ed., *Part-Time Graduate and Professional Study in the Metropolitan Area*, 1974; paper presented at NATO symposium, *Development of a Prototype Computer-Based Testing and Assessment System*, with E. Anastasio, 1985; *Succeeding at Mercer: A Do-it-Yourself Guide to Effective Study Skills*, 1990.

Peggy Sexton-Isaac
1500 East Pusch Wilderness Drive, #3105, Oro Valley, AZ 85737, (520) 297–3068. b. New York, NY, June 10, 1943. e. Georgetown U. Sch. of Nursing, B.S.N., 1961–65; TC, M.A., 1968–70; Northern Arizona U., Ed.D., 1981–89.

Employment: Navajo CC, 1970–71 and 1976–77; Pima CC, 1972–76 and 1991–97; Cochise Coll., 1979–86; Lewis-Clark State Coll., 1986–91.

Publications: dissertation, *Arizona Community College Instr.s' Attitudes Towards and Perceptions of Adult Learners*, 1989.

Sonya Shapiro
34 Scenic Drive, Suffern, NY 10901, (845) 354–1136, soshapiro@aol.com; partner and corp. officer, 21 Perlman Drive, Spring Valley, NY 10977, (845) 371–2100. b. New York, NY, May 17, 1927. e. NYU, B.A., 1948, M.A., 1949; Long Island U., M.S., 1977; TC, Ed.D, 1979; post-doctoral work, TC and Pace U.; Harvard, "Program on Negotiation for Senior Executives."

Employment: special educ. teacher, NYC Board of Educ., 1949–54; parent advocate, East Ramapo Sch. District, 1954–76; Rockland CC, SUNY, career and educ. counselor, 1975–79, psych. instr., 1976–79; dir. educ. and career service, Westchester Educ. Brokering Service, Cornell U., 1979–81; assoc. dean, Pace U., 1981–85; assoc. dean and prof., NYC Technical Coll., CUNY, 1985–89; SVP corp. development and admin., North American Training Services, Inc., NY, 1989–92; dir. adult educ. and business services, Rockland County Board of Cooperative Educ. Services, 1992–2000.

Publications: co-author, "The Summer Scholar" and "New Routes to a College Degree: Non-Traditional Ways to Earn a Degree," *New York Magazine*; *Adult Career Counseling Manual*, NY State Educ. Dept.

Walter E. Sindlinger
b. Gnadhutton, Ohio, February 14, 1914. d. June 16, 1955. e. Ohio State University, AB, 1936; Teachers College, MA, 1939; Ed.D., 1953.

Employment: teaching experience as an English instructor and guidance counselor in Pickerton and Galion, Ohio, public schools; World War II service in the Armed Forces Institute, principally as chief of the accreditation at the University of Rome. After the war, several years in media research; Instructor in English and guidance counselor, Orange County CC, 1950, dean, 1952–1956, with periods of leave for teaching and research at TC; community-college specialist, U. of Michigan, 1957–1958; dir. of TC Community Coll. Center, 1960; prof., TC, 1963; two terms as chair of Department of Higher and Adult Education, 1968–70 and 1974–79.

Cheryl M. Smith
3 Denise Street, Massapequa, NY 11758, (516) 541–4522, csmith@york.cuny.edu; asst. VP for academic affairs, York Coll., CUNY, 94–20 Guy R. Brewer Boulevard, Jamaica, NY 11451. b. Georgetown, Guyana. e. Downstate Medical Center, SUNY, B.S.; Hunter Coll., M.S./M.P.H.; TC, M.Ed., Ed.D.

Employment: radiological sciences and technology educ., NYC Technical Coll., 1978–94.

Publications: "The Use of Stress Reduction Training with Radiological Technology Students," *Quarterly Journal of Human Behavior*, 1987; conference proceedings manual, "Healing and Socialization in the Multi-Cultural Classroom," CUNY Assoc. of Writing Supervisors, 1990.

Charles S. Soper
5684 Germany Road, Verona, NY 13478–3804, (315) 363–1494. b. Newark, NY, Apr. 3, 1939. e. New Paltz State Teacher's Coll., 1959–60; Dutchess CC, NY, A.A.S., 1960–62; TC, B.S., 1962–64, M.Ed., 1964–66.

Employment: clinical seminar instr., psychological and mental health, New York Hosp., 1962–63; clinical seminar instr., NY State Psychiatric Hosp., 1963–64; psychiatric, mental health, pediatric nursing, Creedmoor State Hosp., 1964–66; consultant, instr., and chair, dept. of nursing educ., Midway Jr. Coll., 1966–70 (created, developed and implemented two-yr. nursing program); asst. prof., Kingsborough CC, 1970–72.

Katherine C. Southwick
30 Crescent Road, Poughkeepsie, NY 12601–4413, (845) 454–2274; prof. emerita, Dutchess CC. b. Dobbs Ferry, NY, Oct. 11, 1923. e. Hudson River State Hosp., NY, R.N., 1944; TC, B.S., 1968, Ed.M., 1974.
Employment: prof., Dutchess CC, NY, 1969–91 (prog. chair, 2 yrs., dept. head, 1 yr.); developed and implemented one of the first perceptorship programs for senior nursing students within community colleges.

Stuart Steiner
33 Woodcrest Drive, Batavia, NY 14020, (716) 343–2617, ssteiner@genesee.suny.edu; pres., Genesee CC, 1 College Road, Batavia, NY 14020. e. Baltimore Jr. Coll., A.A.; U. of Maryland, B.S.; Florida State U., graduate certificate in social work; UPenn, M.S.W.; U. of Baltimore, J.D.; TC, M.A., Ed.D.
Employment: caseworker, supervisor, dir. of juvenile court services, Baltimore City Dept. of Social Services, 1959–64; faculty, CC of Baltimore, 1963–67; dir. of metropolitan Baltimore information and referral services, Health and Welfare Council of Metropolitan Baltimore, 1964–65; dir. of admissions and placement, Harford CC, MD, 1965–67; adjunct faculty, Rochester Institute of Technology, 1974–82; adjunct faculty, SUNY Buffalo, 1977–present; visiting prof., Catholic U., 1979; Genesee CC, dean of students, 1967–68, dean of instruction/exec.dean, 1968–75, pres., 1975–present; deputy to chancellor of community colleges, SUNY, 1985; acting pres., FIT, 1997–98; received Kellogg Fellowship in Community College Administration, TC.
Publications: book review, *The Community College Presidency*, in *Higher Education: The International Journal of Higher Education and Educational Planning*, 1987; "SUNY—The 'Systemless' System,"

Voices of Leadership, 1994; "Community Colleges of the Nineties: Living on the Fiscal Edge," in *Higher Education in Turmoil: The Case of New York State and Natural Prospect for Change*, 1995.

Lorelei V. Stocker
4814 Rollingtop Road, Ellicott City, MD 21043, (410) 465–5140. b. New York, NY, June 1, 1932. e. Presbyterian Hosp. Sch. of Nursing, 1950–53; TC, B.S., 1955–57; U. of Maryland, M.S., 1965–66, M.S., 1969–70.
Employment: medical/surgical nurse, Springfield Hosp., MA, 1957–58; assoc. prof., Catonsville CC, MD, 1965–92.
Publications: Pediatric Nursing Modules, 1982–92.

Jeane S. Stockheim
9 Island Avenue, #1607, Miami Beach, FL 33139, (305) 672–8922, jstockheim@aol.com. e. sr. hosp. diploma, 1929–32; NYU, B.S., 1940–46; Columbia, M.A., 1954; Hunter Coll., special educ., 1964.
Employment: instr., exec. medical assistants, Brooklyn CC, 1960–62.

Rose Carol Strohmann
135 Lake Point Drive, League City, TX 77573, rosestrohmann@aol.com, dir. nursing educ., Health Education Resources–International, 10407 Barwood Drive, Houston, TX, 77043. b. New York, NY, June 4, 1922. e. Creedmoor State Hosp. Sch. of Nursing, diploma; TC, B.S., 1952; U. of Houston, certificate, hosp. admin., organization, and supervision, 1967, M.Ed., 1969; Texas A & M, certificate, inservice educ. and analysis and course making for health occupations, 1974; U. Texas Sch. of Public Health, Dr.P.H., 1975.
Employment: psych. nurse, Veterans Admin. Hosp., TX, 1953–54; Jefferson Davis Hosp., TX, labor and delivery room nurse, 1957–60, maternal/child health supervisor and instr., 1960–61, asst. dir. of nursing services, 1961–63; dir. of nursing service, Harris County Hosp. District, 1963–67; public health nurse, City of Houston Dept. of Health, 1967–69; instr., nursing educ., San Jacinto Coll., TX, 1969–77; assoc. prof. and acting chair of dept. of psychiatric/community health, Prairie View A & M U. Coll. of Nursing, TX, 1977–78; nurse intern co-

ord., St. Joseph Hosp. Medical Center, TX, 1978–83; dir. nursing educ., Health Education Resources—International, TX, 1983–present; adjunct faculty, San Jacinto Coll., 1983–present; adjunct faculty, Houston CC, 1983–present.

Publications: Procedure Workbook for Psychiatric Attendants, 1948; "Allied Health Manpower: The Ladder Concept on the Education of Nursing Service Personnel," *Texas Urban Development Commission— Policies for the Future*, 1971; "Clinical Experience: Vital to Nursing Education," *Nursing Outlook*, 1977.

Charlotte (Offhouse) Sun
PO Box 9224, Moscow, ID 83843–1724, (208) 285–0123; dir., Genesee Valley Daoist Hermitage (same as home address). b. Paterson, NJ, May 5, 1941. e. St. Luke's Hosp. Sch. of Nursing, NY, diploma, 1962; Columbia, B.S., 1966; Holy Names Coll., CA, M.Ed., 1973; Hangzhou U., China, doctoral studies, 1980; California Institute of Integral Studies, Ph.D., 1985.

Employment: self-employed nurse, NY, 1962–66; PHN office coord., private practice, CA, 1966–67; patient care coord. and counselor, Pacific Heights Convalescent Hosp., CA, 1967–70; patient care coord. and part owner, Pacific Heights Home Health Center, 1968–69; nurse consultant, Veterans Admin. Hosp., 1968–78; extension fac. member, Chabot Coll., Solano Coll., Holy Names Coll., 1970–86; retirement hotel mgr., CA, 1972; assoc. project dir., regional medical programs, UC San Francisco, 1970–73; private consultant, long-term care facilities, 1972–86; Medical Manors Group, CA, admin. and part owner, 1974–76, patient care coord., 1976–77; dir. staff development and part owner, The Living Centers Management Co., CA, 1977–85; consultant, Oriental Longevity Sciences Research Center, China, 1984–88; fac., John F. Kennedy U., 1985–89; private practic in acupressure and Daoism, 1985–present; dir., Daoist Longevity Center, 1987–93; Integral Health Studies Program, found. and dir., 1988–93, adjunct fac., 1993–present; dir., Genesee Valley Daoist Hermitage, ID, 1993–present; fac., Moscow Sch. of Massage, ID, 1995–present.

Publications: "Extended Care," *Journal of Nursing Administration*, 1971; *Extended Care: Guidelines for Patient Care Coordination and Counseling*, 1974.

Marian Sussna
111 East 30th Street, New York, NY 10016, (212) 683–5304, mariansussna@cs.com. b. Oct. 18, 1925, Glens Falls, NY. e. Ohio State, 1944; SUNY Albany, 1947; TC, M.A., 1955.

Employment: Warrensburg HS, NY, 1947–49; Pratt Business Sch. and Eron Prep., NY, 1949–52; NY City CC, 1953–56; Princeton HS, 1964–66; Lawrence Sch., NJ, 1966–68; Hamilton Township Sch., 1972–87.

Barbara Hanaford Sykes
230 East Main Street, Ionia, MI 48846, (616) 527–3654, bhsykes@aol.com. b. Canton, China, Jan. 26, 1933. e. Evanston Hosp. Sch. of Nursing, 1951–54; TC, B.S., 1956, M.A., 1959.

Employment: nursing instr., Columbia U., 1956–59; nursing instr., TC, 1959–61, worked with Kellogg Foundation Grant to prepare teachers for community-college nursing programs.

Rosa H. Tate
47 North Road, White Plains, NY 10603, (914) 948–8156. b. VA, Dec. 24, 1921. e. valedictorian, Harlem Hosp. Sch. of Nursing, 1944; Columbia, B.S., 1964; TC, M.A., 1967, permanent sch. nurse and teacher certification, 1968; Cornell, intensified instr. training certificate, 1968.

Employment: Harlem Hosp. Sch. of Nursing, instr., 1964–69, chair, MCH program, 1966–69; Bronx CC, instr., 1969–71, asst. nursing prof., 1971, tenure, 1974, assoc. nursing prof., 1976–88, adjunct prof., 1989–95.

Marie R. Traetta
162 Drisler Avenue, White Plains, NY 10607. b. New York, NY, Apr. 30, 1931. e. Misericordia Hosp. Sch. of Nursing, 1952; TC, B.S., 1958, M.A., 1962, M.Ed., 1969; Fordham, Ed.D., 1985.

Employment: nurse, 1952–58; teacher and admin., Rockland CC, SUNY, 1958–95; Queensborough CC, CUNY, 1968–95.

Patricia A. Tumminia
5911 Oak Ridge Court, Burke, VA 22015, (703) 250–9716; prof. of nursing, Northern Virginia CC, 8333 Little River Turnpike, Annandale,

VA 22003. b. New York, NY, Dec. 10, 1940. e. Columbia, B.S.N., 1965; TC, M.A., 1967, Ed.M., 1976; George Mason, doctorate of arts, 1997.

Employment: instr., medical and surgical nursing, Alexandria Sch. of Nursing, 1967–72; nursing prof., Northern Virginia CC, 1972–present.

Publications: "Teaching Problems and Strategies with Male Nursing Students," *Nurse Educator*, 1981; co-author, "Teaching the Nursing Disabled Nursing Student," *Nurse Educator*, 1993; "Education of Nursing Students with Special Needs," *Journal of Nursing Education*, 1996.

M. Gladys Updegrove
1900A Ravine Road, #221, Williamsport, PA 17701, (570) 327–8149. b. Herndon, PA, Sept. 1, 1916. e. Williamsport Hosp. Sch. of Nursing, 1937; coursework in pediatrics, Children's Hosp., PA, 1939; TC, B.S., 1957, M.A., 1962.

Employment: supervisor of pediatrics and instr., Harrisburg Hosp., 1952–62; Williamsport Hosp., supervisor of pediatrics and instr., 1940–52, supervisor of fundamentals of nursing, 1962, asst. dir. of nursing service, 1963–79, dir. of nursing service, 1979–81.

Harold M. Updike
2452 Brazilia Drive, #24, Clearwater, FL 33763–3706, (727) 797–2845. b. Ithaca, NY, Feb. 16, 1929. e. U. of Buffalo, SUNY, B.S., 1954; TC, M.A., 1970.

Employment: former dir. of nursing at two Brooklyn hospitals, incorporated local community colleges as part of the training curriculum.

Publications: Forty Years and Counting: A Nurse's Story; Around the World in Twenty Years; Emergency; Ithaca; Amazing People I have Known; The Art of Science and Communication, in progress.

Judy Ann Valyo
1275 15th Street, #12I, Fort Lee, NJ 07024–1926, (201) 224–3605, valyo@njit.edu; dean of freshman studies, NJ Institute of Technology, Newark, NJ 07024. b. Queens, NY, Mar. 25, 1945. e. Molloy Coll., B.A., 1963–67; NYU, M.A., 1967–69; TC, Ed.D., 1977–85.

Employment: resident life, Hofstra U., 1969–72; student activities, Ramapo Coll., 1972–76; student center, advising, Rockland CC,

1976–81; NJ Institute of Technology, dean of students, 1981–90, dean of freshman studies, 1990–present.

Elizabeth F. Wagoner
241 Jefferis Road, Downington, PA 19335, (610) 942–3923, wagoner2@bigplanet.net. b. Bronx, NY, Dec. 22, 1934. e. White Plains Hosp. Sch. of Nursing, 1952–55; Ohio State, B.S.N., 1955–57; TC, M.A., 1963; Rutgers, Ed.D., 1979.
Employment: Nassau CC, 1962–65.

Robina Hastie Wertalik
64 Reider Road, Edison, NJ 08817–2805, (732) 549–8462. b. New York, NY, May 29, 1929. e. TC, B.S., 1959; NYU, M.A., 1978.

LaZelle Westbrook
5038 Severance Drive, San Jose, CA 95136–2743, ladylaz@worldnet. att.net. b. Austin, TX, Oct. 24, 1934. e. UC Berkeley, nursing, 1951–56; TC, M.A., 1963.
Employment: nursing instr., Norfolk Div. of Virginia State Coll., 1963–64; nursing instr., San Jose City Coll., 1964–75; Evergree Valley Coll., CA, nursing instr., 1975–94, dir. nursing educ., 1995–2001.

Sidney James White
b. New York, NY, May 1, 1919. d. April 16, 1982. e. U of Toledo, B.B.A; Columbia U, M.S.; TC, Ed.D.
Employment: asst. to secretary treasurer and VP of admin., Stein Hall Co., NY, 1952–55; owner, American Academic Supply Co., NY, 1955–58; VP, Cox Sons & Vining, Inc., NY, 1959–65; accounting and business instr., Suffolk County CC, NY, 1965–67; prof. of business, Queensborough CC, NY, 1967–82.

D. Camilla Wygan
160 Academy Street, #K1, Poughkeepsie, NY 12601, (845) 454–0044; adjunct instr., Dutchess CC, Pendell Road, Poughkeepsie, NY 12601. b. New York, NY, Apr. 10, 1932. e. American U., B.S., 1953; Coll. of New Rochelle, M.S.Ed., 1973; TC, Ed.D., 1992.

Employment: developmental learning specialist, Wappmyers Central sch. district, 1973–76; dir., learning resources, Culinary Institute of America, 1976–82; dir. institutional advancement, Dutchess CC, 1982–87; VP institutional advancement, Rockland CC, 1987–90; exec. dir., Sarah Wells Girl Scouts Council, 1990–97; adjunct instr., behavioral sciences, Dutchess CC, 1997–present.

Estelle Lurie Yahes
6 Quince Lane, Suffern, NY 10901–3304, (845) 354–9236, estelle-meir@msn.com; prof. nursing, SUNY Rockland CC, 145 College Road, Suffern, NY 10901, eyahes@sunyrockland.edu. b. Bronx, NY, Apr. 26, 1948. e. Hunter, Bellevue, NY, B.S.N., 1969; TC, M.A., 1978.

Employment: staff team leader, NYU Medical Center, 1969–71; nurse mgr., Albert Einstein Coll. of Medicine, NY, 1971–73; faculty lecturer and instr., St. Joseph's Hosp., NY, 1973–75; adjunct clinical instr., Pace U., NY, 1975–82; Rockland CC, NY, adjunct clinical instr., 1975–82, acting dean, lifelong learning, 1986, project dir., Center for Health and Health Professionals, 1988–90, interim dir., Center for Workforce Development and Continuing Educ., 1997, coord. of continuing educ. for health professionals, 1980–2000, nursing prof., 2000–present.

Publications: "Enculturation of Foreign Nurse Graduates: An Integrated Model," *Journal of Continuing Education in Nursing,* with A. Dunn, 1996.

Dale A. Young
2341 Canton Road, Akron, OH 44312, (330) 699–2341; minister of visitation, First Grace United Church of Christ, 350 South Portage Path, Akron, OH 44320, (330) 762–8469. b. Springfield Township, OH, June 8, 1916. e. Kent State, 1940; Oberlin, 1953; TC, M.A., 1954, Ed.D., 1960.

Employment: athletic coach and social studies teacher, Springfield Township HS, OH (3 yrs.); summer pastor, Dixon, IL; attended seminars and performed field studies of education in Africa and Russia; dean of students, Shepherd Coll., WV (4 yrs.); dean of men's office, Ohio State U. (3 yrs.); assoc. acad. dean, Malone Coll., OH (14 yrs.); dir. institutional research and planning, Stark State Coll. of Technology,

OH (17 yrs.); currently, minister of visitation, First Grace United Church of Christ.

Publications: wrote several articles for the Ohio Commission on Aging, The Project for Academic Excellence; contributed many articles to various religious newsletters; authored a history of the Frederick Young family (1998).

Chris Ypsilanti

238 2nd Road, Key Largo, FL 33037, ypsilach@yahoo.com; dir., Upper Keys Center, PO Drawer 600, Tavernier, FL 33070. b. New York, NY, Feb. 27, 1949. e. Westchester CC, 1967–69; Hofstra, 1969–71; TC, M.A., 1978–81; Nova U., 1987–91.

Employment: NYC adult basic educ. (4 yrs.); adult educ. instr., Miccosukee Tribe Indians (3 yrs.); dir., Florida Keys CC (16 yrs.).

Kristin P. Zebrowski

20 Fay Road, New City, NY 10956–3329, (845) 638–1257, kzebrowski@bankstreet.edu; admin. coord., Bank Street Coll. of Educ. Graduate Sch., 610 West 112th Street, New York, NY 10025–1898. b. Suffern, NY, July 21, 1970. e. Skidmore Coll., B.A., 1992; Pace U., J.D., 1997; TC, M.A., 1998.

Employment: Rockland CC, acting dir., office of student involvement, 1996–97, admin. of student activities, 1997; career services, List Coll. of the Jewish Theological Seminary of America, 1997–98; Bank Street Coll. of Education Graduate Sch., admin. coord. for academic affairs, 1999–2000, admin. coord. for the Graduate Sch., 2000–present.

Andrew Zeitlin

61 West Waukena Avenue, Oceanside, NY 11572–5021, (516) 678–6457, azeitlin@kbcc.cuny.edu; prof. and chair, biological sciences, Kingsborough CC, 2001 Oriental Boulevard, Brooklyn, NY 11235. b. Brooklyn, NY, Aug. 14, 1940. e. Long Island U., B.S., 1963; TC, Ed.M., 1987, Ed.D., 1988.

Appendix B

DISSERTATIONS LIST

The following are dissertations on a wide variety of community college topics written by Teachers College graduate students as part of their requirement for completion of the Doctor of Education degree.

Frank Aleman
The Nontransfer Transfer Student, June 1976
  dissertation committee: Harland Bloland, sponsor; Walter Sindlinger

Virginia Opie Allen
A Design for a New Educational Option in Associate Degree Nursing,
January 1978
  dissertation committee: Alice R. Rines, sponsor; Walter E. Sindlinger

Cynthia Ofosua Atanda
Evaluation of a GED Program, May 1995
  dissertation committee: Marvin Sontag, sponsor; Richard M. Wolf

Marie-Claire Barthelemy
An Updated Data Processing Curriculum: Recommendations for a Two-Year College, May 1992
  dissertation committee: Robert P. Taylor, sponsor; J. Philip Smith

Helen Catherine Blankenship
Coaching Teachers: Staff Development in a Postsecondary Technical and Trade School, October 1990
  dissertation committee: Thurston Atkins, sponsor; William Yakowicz

Edward Marvin Bostick
A Remedial and Developmental Reading Program in a Community College: Students' Opinions and Recommendations for Program Development, January 1989
  dissertation committee: Thomas Leemon, sponsor; Mary Mowrey Raddock

Kathryn Winifred Cafferty
The Role of the Administrator of the Nursing Program in the Community-Junior College, October 1959
  dissertation committee: Mildred L. Montag, sponsor; Ralph R. Field; Thad L. Hungate

Peter Ching-Tai Chiu
Post-Secondary Vocational-Technical Education in Pennsylvania: A Case Study of the Conflict Between Community Colleges and Area Vocational-Technical Schools, April 1975
  dissertation committee: Walter E. Sindlinger, sponsor; Harland G. Bloland

Henry Leroy Cody
Considerations for Textbook Selection for Community Colleges, October 1978
  dissertation committee: Phil C. Lange, sponsor; William E. Hug

Edward Anthony Colozzi
Did they Leave for the Best of Reasons? A Study of Persisters and Dropouts in an Open Admissions Community College, September 1973
  dissertation committee: Michael Brick, sponsor; Gordon Darkenwald

Leontina A. Diaz
The Relation of Rule Retention and Rule Transfer to the Algebra Performance of Minority Community College Students, September 1990
  dissertation committee: Bruce A. Vogeli, sponsor; Philip Smith

Loretta DiLorenzo
A Proposed New Model of the Innovation Process in an Educational Organization: A Community College Case Study, May 1994
  dissertation committee: L. Lee Knefelkamp, sponsor; Dawn Person

Diane Elizabeth Ducat
Cooperative Education, Self-Concept, and Occupational Concept for Community College Students, 1979
  dissertation committee: Roger A. Myers, sponsor; Jean P. Jordaan; Richard H. Lindeman

Philip Arthur Fey
In Search of Community: An Examination of Levels of Interrelatedness Between the Community College and its Community, September 1976
  dissertation committee: Walter E. Sindlinger, sponsor; David E. Wilder

Sandra B. Fielo
Role Perception, Importance of Personal Autonomy, and Frequency of Informal Grievance Initiation Reported by Nurse-Teachers in Public Community Colleges Governed by Negotiated Contracts in the State of New Jersey, November 1977
  dissertation committee: Robert Piemonte, sponsor; Elizabeth Maloney

Donald Fitzgerald
Image of the Public Community Colleges in Massachusetts, May 1971
  dissertation committee: Walter E. Sindlinger, sponsor; Richard Videbeck

James Joseph Fitzpatrick
Perceptions of Adult Learning in Multinational Maritime Continuing Higher Education: A Case Study Emphasizing the Views of Maritime Faculty, February 1996
    dissertation committee: Philip Fey, sponsor; William Vericker

Henry Seth Flax
From Community College to College Community: Transfer Counselors and the Community College Transfer Opportunity Program, May 1996
    dissertation committee: Dawn R. Person, sponsor; Joseph N. Hankin

Barry Freeman
A Study of the Efficacy of a Developmental Instruction Design for Non-Traditional Adult Learners, May 1994
    dissertation committee: L. Lee Knefelkamp, sponsor; Harvey Kaye

Mildred Garcia
Community College Student Presence: A Field Application of the Tinto Model, May 1987
    dissertation committee: Richard Birnbaum, sponsor; Richard E. Anderson

June L. Gaston
Student Reluctance/Difficulty with Calculator Use in Community College Mathematics Courses, May 1990
    dissertation committee: J. Philip Smith, sponsor; Paul Rosenbloom

Ronald Hal Gerwin
Role of the Department Chairperson in the Administration of Health Education Programs in Community Colleges, July 1977
    dissertation committee: James L. Malfetti, sponsor; Kenneth J. Simon

David Glenday
The Evaluation of Alternate Plans for Financing Operational Costs of Community Colleges in New York State, October 1961
    dissertation committee: John W. Polley, sponsor; Harold F. Clark

Lassar G. Gotkin
An Evaluation of the Nursing Performance of the Graduates of the Experimental Nursing Programs in Junior and Community Colleges, May 1958
    dissertation committee: Ralph R. Fields, sponsor; Elizabeth Hagen; Mildred Montag

Charles Wayne Hall
The Position and Function of the State Officer Responsible for Public Community-Junior College Education, November 1966
    dissertation committee: Ralph R. Fields, sponsor; Walter E. Sindlinger

Audrey W. Harrigan
Integrated Skills Reinforcement, March 1990
    dissertation committee: Martin Finkelstein, sponsor; Thomas Leemon

Maria Antonia Irizarry
A Proposed Model for a Bilingual Approach Mode of Instruction, at the Two Year College Level (Spanish-English), December 1976
    dissertation committee: Mordecai S. Rubin, sponsor; Annette Baslaw

Nancy Vazac Jackson
A Survey of Part-Time Faculty in Baccalaureate Schools of Nursing and Their Learning Needs, February 1996
    dissertation committee: Marie O'Toole, sponsor; Sheila Melli; Jane Rogers

Paul L. Johnson
Community College Education: A Book of Readings, August 1951
    dissertation committee: Karl W. Bigelow, sponsor; Paul L. Essert; Ralph R. Fields

Marilyn Keener
Academic Role Enactment and the Perception of the Prestige and Acceptance of Faculty Members in Nursing in Selected Community Colleges in Illinois, October 1982

dissertation committee: Elizabeth Maloney, sponsor; Andrea O'Connor

Isabel W. Kimmel
Comments on Comments on Comments: Teacher Comments from Student Perspectives, 1996
    dissertation committee: Lucy McCormick Calkins, sponsor; Barbara Kiefer

Robert E. Kinsinger
Student Personnel Factors in Community College Education, March 1958
    dissertation committee: Raymond A. Patouillet, sponsor; Paul G. Bulger; Mildred L. Montag

John G. Klinzing
A Comparison of the Perceptions of New Jersey Community College Trustees and Presidents on Trustee Responsibilities and Effectiveness, July 1973
    dissertation committee: Walter Sindlinger, sponsor; Harland Bloland; Gordon Darkenwald

Robert William Kochenour
A Study of the Need for and Feasibility of Establishing a Community College in Franklin County, Pennsylvania, May 1960
    dissertation committee: William P. Anderson, sponsor; Ralph R. Fields; Walter E. Sindlinger

Martin Jeffrey Lecker
Integrated Skills Reinforcement in Business Communications at Rockland Community College, April 1990
    dissertation committee: Thomas Leemon, sponsor; Mary Mowrey-Raddock

Jenni Kye Ju Lee-Kim
The Labor Market Returns to Community College Education as Evidenced in the MIS EDD/UI Wage Data, 1998

dissertation committee: Thomas Bailey, sponsor; Phoebus Dhrymes; Robert Crain

Seyma Louise Ocko Levine
Study Circles: A Mode of Learning for Older Adults in the Community College Setting, October 1994
    dissertation committee: Victoria J. Marsick, sponsor; Walter E. Sindlinger

Marguerite Manning
Teacher Aide Training in Community Colleges, August 1975
    dissertation committee: Walter E. Sindlinger, sponsor; Richard Videbeck

Linda Aneha Marcel
A Lecture Performance at Bergen Community College to Promote Community Awareness of Local Composers, May 1994
    dissertation committee: Robert Pace, sponsor; Lenore Pogonowski

Salvatore Thomas Martino
Integrated Skills Reinforcement in Radiologic Technology at Hostos Community College, May 1991
    dissertation committee: Thomas Leemon, sponsor; Mary Mowrey-Raddock

Judith Martin-Wambu
Case Studies of Nine Community College Good Writers/Poor Readers, October 1988
    dissertation committee: Dorothy S. Strickland, sponsor; Winthrop R. Adkins

Daniel Maysonet
Improving Achievement in College Remedial Mathematics with the Hand-Held Calculator, May 1990
    dissertation committee: Bruce R. Vogeli, sponsor; Paul C. Rosenbloom; J. Philip Smith

Margaret McAuliffe
Making Public Policy Decisions Sensitive to the Needs of Students and Community Colleges: The Stafford Loan Case Consumer Information Legislation, September 1991
   dissertation committee: Thomas Leemon; Mary Mowrey-Raddock

Helen Marie McCabe
Cooperative Education in the Community College: A Critical Analysis, 1980
   dissertation committee: Lambros Comitas, sponsor; Maxine Greene; Philip H. Phenix

Marjorie McDonough
An Assessment of Critical Thinking at the Community College Level, May 1997
   dissertation committee: Joseph Hankin, sponsor; Philip Fey

Andrew Lee Meyer
Facilitating Adult Learning Through Continuing Education: A Case Study of Carroll Community College, 1989
   dissertation committee: Philip A. Fey, sponsor; Elizabeth S. Kasl

Dorothy Wilkes Miller
Structure and Processes of Two Community College Offices: A Contingency Approach, January 1991
   dissertation committee: Robert Birnbaum, sponsor; Richard E. Anderson

Estelle L. Miller
Fears Expressed by Female Reentry Students at an Urban Community College: A Qualitative Study, August 1997
   dissertation committee: Franceska Smith, sponsor; Victoria Marsick

Edward Dickie Mills
Determining the Image of a Community College Held by Voters, April 1969

dissertation committee: Walter E. Sindlinger, sponsor; Sloan R. Wayland

Kerwin Rene Nollez
Gatekeepers of Reading and Their Impact on Students' Success, February 1995
    dissertation committee: L. Lee Knefelkamp, sponsor; Harvey Kay

Elizabeth N. Norton
An Evaluation of the Academic Success of the 1966 and 1967 Pre-Technical Graduates at Three Public Community Colleges of the City University of New York, May 1970
    dissertation committee: Michael Brick, sponsor; Alan Knox

Yuko Otomo
The Relationship of Computer Anxiety, Mathematics Anxiety, Trait Anxiety, Test Anxiety, Gender, and Demographic Characteristics Among Community College Students, May 1998
    dissertation committee: Bruce R. Vogeli, sponsor; J. Philip Smith

Charlene Patricia Pappin
A Descriptive Study of Implementation of Specific Programmed Materials for Junior College Arithmetic Studies, September 1973
    dissertation committee: Bruce R. Vogeli, sponsor; Paul V. Robinson

J. Allen Pawling
An Approach to the Development of a Community Arts Center, May 1959
    dissertation committee: E. Ziegfeld, sponsor; A. R. Young

Robert Patrick Pedersen
The Origins and Development of the Early Public Junior College: 1900–1940, 2000
    dissertation committee: Douglas N. Sloan, sponsor; Joseph N. Hankin; Harold S. Wechsler

Eileen Brown Pennino
Integrated Skills Reinforcement Applied to Western Civilization Content in a Community College, May 1991
   dissertation committee: Thomas A. Leemon, sponsor; Mary Mowrey-Raddock

Michael Joel Perlin
The Effects of an Intensive Versus Extensive Thirty-Hour Health Education Course Upon Students' Attitudes Toward and Knowledge in Health Education in an Urban Community College, May 1981
   dissertation committee: Kenneth J. Simon, sponsor; James L. Malfetti

Geraldine Pozzi-Galluzi
Planning Survey for the Development of HIV/AIDS Programs for Community College Students, May 1994
   dissertation committee: John P. Allegrante, sponsor; Robert Crain

Louise Styche Rainis
A Comparative Analysis of Contracted Training Programs with Recommendations for Dundalk Community College, October 1989
   dissertation committee: Jack Mezirow, sponsor; Walter Sindlinger

Emory Webster Rarig Jr.
Administrative Practices in Institutional Long-Range Planning in Community and Junior Colleges, June 1968
   dissertation committee: Walter E. Sindlinger, sponsor; Michael Brick

Judith F. Raulf
An Insitutional Evaluation of Perceptions and Expectations of Prior Learning Assessment Programs, April 1992
   dissertation committee: Elizabeth Kasl, sponsor; Stephen Brookfield

Kathleen Marie Rice
The Impact of Contracting Courses Upon the Decision-Making Behavior of Adult Students, January 1976
   dissertation committee: W. Max Wise, sponsor; Roger A. Myers

Gwendolyn D. Roundtree
The Evaluation of the Vassar College Exploring Transfer Program, October 1995
  dissertation committee: Dawn Person, sponsor; Kathleen Loughlin

Carol J. Russett
Factors That Facilitate or Impede Informal Workplace Learning Among Faculty in a Large Suburban New York State Community College, March 1991
  dissertation committee: Jack Mezirow, sponsor; Walter Sindlinger

Mildred S. Schmidt
Factors Which Have Led to or Deterred the Establishment of Associate Degree Programs in Nursing in Community Junior Colleges, August 1965
  dissertation committee: Mildred L. Montag, sponsor; Walter E. Sindlinger

Charles J. Schulze Jr.
The Role of the Community College President in Successful Fundraising, October 1991
  dissertation committee: Richard Anderson, sponsor; Joseph Hankin

Barbara Christy Benson Shellhouse
An Analysis of Community College Music Departments in the State of Illinois, October 1990
  dissertation committee: Harold F. Abeles, sponsor; Robert Pace

Walter Eugene Sindlinger
Experimentation in Education for Nursing at Orange County Community College, 1956
  dissertation committee: Ralph M. Fields, major adviser; Margaret Lindsey; Mildred L. Montag

Michael Steven Slifer
Correlates of Decision-Making Styles, February 1994
  dissertation committee: Peter C. Cairo, sponsor; Roger A. Myers

Cheryl M. Smith
Integrated Skills Reinforcement in Radiation Biology, May 1990
  dissertation committee: Thomas A. Leemon, sponsor; Mary
  Mowrey-Raddock

Donald Henry Smith
Assessing the Image of a Community College Held in High School Seniors, April 1969
  dissertation committee: Walter E. Sindlinger, sponsor; Sloan
  R. Wayland

Ellen Weinstein Smith
Occupational Program Planning at New Jersey Community Colleges: Manpower Needs Determination Processes, April 1975
  dissertation committee: W. Max Wise, sponsor; Walter E. Sindlinger

Peter W. Smith
Local Government and the Community College: A Case Study, March 1970
  dissertation committee: Michael Brick, sponsor; Walter Sindlinger

Ernest Martin Sobel
Community College Faculty Participation in Academic Decision Making, July 1971
  dissertation committee: Michael Brick, sponsor; Walter E. Sindlinger

Carol L. Solon
Whole Language: A Promising Approach to Teaching Reading to Underprepared Community College Students, May 1991
  dissertation committee: Thomas A. Leemon, sponsor; Mary
  Mowrey-Raddock

Martin Tarcher
The Italian Institute for Community Centers: A Social Experiment in Italy, May 1958
  dissertation committee: Donald G. Tewksbury, sponsor; Mark Flapan; Wilbur C. Hallenbeck

Gwen Tolliver-Luster
An Evaluation of an Instructional Design in an Introductory Principles of Marketing Class, September 1993
    dissertation committee: L. Lee Knefelkamp, sponsor; Dawn Person

Thomas Edward Topping
An Institutional Evaluation of Perceptions and Expectations of Prior Learning Assessment Options, May 1996
    dissertation committee: Elizabeth Kasl, sponsor; Philip Fey

Carl Urbont
The Avowed and Operating Purposes of the Contemporary Jewish Community Center Movement, April 1966
    dissertation committee: Sloan R. Wayland, sponsor; Leah M. Rich; Ralph B. Spence

Sidney James White
The Relationship of Selected Factors to Choice of Curriculum and Career: A Comparative Study of Terminal and Transfer Accounting Program Students in Three Urban, Public Community Colleges, February 1974
    dissertation committee: W. Max Wise, sponsor; A. Harry Passow

Renee Sandra Woloshin
Improving the Prediction of Academic Persistence and Performance in Community Colleges for Minority Students by the Addition of Nonintellective Variables to Traditional Intellective Measures, 1981
    dissertation committee: Miriam L. Goldberg, sponsor; Richard M. Wolf

Richard George Wright
Professionalization of Administrators: Developments in the Community College Field, 1917 to 1975, May 1976
    dissertation committee: Harland G. Bloland, sponsor; Walter E. Sindlinger

Dorothy Camilla Reznikoff Wygan
The Effect of Community Colleges Upon Students and Their Persistence, May 1992
　　dissertation committee: Thomas Leemon, sponsor; Mary Mowrey-Raddock

About the Authors

Martin S. Quigley (Ed.D., 1975) spent a quarter century in film trade journalism as a reporter, reviewer, editor, and publisher before starting studies at Teachers College, where his principal dissertation sponsors were Donna Shalala and Walter E. Sindlinger. His dissertation was an early study in the politics of higher education: "The Government Relations of Five Universities in Washington, D.C." From the time of his graduation, Quigley taught higher education subjects to teachers and administrators at Baruch College of the City University of New York, Seton Hall University, and Teachers College, where he was a visiting professor in 1990. His books include *Magic Shadows, The Story of the Origin of Motion Pictures* (1948); *New Screen Techniques* (1953); *Catholic Action in Practice* (1963); *Films in America 1929–1969* (1970); *Peace without Hiroshima: Secret Action in the Vatican in the Spring of 1945* (1980); and *A U.S. Spy in Ireland: The Truth behind Irish "Neutrality" during World War II* (1999). His family includes his wife, Katherine, nine children, and twenty-six grandchildren.

Thomas Bailey is the George and Abby O'Neill Professor of Economics and Education in the Department of International and Transcultural Studies at Teachers College, Columbia University. He is also the director of both the Institute on Education and the Economy and the Community College Research Center. Professor Bailey holds a Ph.D. in labor economics from Massachusetts Institute of Technology and is an expert on the economics of education, educational policy, and the educational and training implications of changes in the workplace. He has served as a consultant to many public agencies and foundations including the U.S. Department of Labor, the U.S. Department of Education, the U.S. Congress Office of Technology Assessment, the Alfred P. Sloan Foundation, the William T. Grant Foundation, and several state and local economic development and educational agencies. His articles have appeared in a wide variety of policy-oriented and academic journals, and he has authored or co-authored books on the employment and training of immigrants and the extent and effects of on the job training. His book, *The Double Helix of Education and the Economy* (1992), written with Sue Berryman, examines the poorly understood link between the needs of the workplace and the contemporary understanding of effective learning. His edited book, *Learning to Work: Employer Involvement in School-to-Work Transition Programs* (1995), analyzes the roles of employers in the education system. His published report, *School to Work for the College Bound*, maintains that the school-to-work model is effective in teaching high-level academic skills and preparing students for college. His most recent book, *Manufacturing Advantage* (2000), written with Eileen Appelbaum, Peter Berg, and Arne Kalleberg, analyzes the effects of high-performance work systems on organizational performance and worker welfare.